# Proclamation 4

Aids for Interpreting
the Lessons of the Church Year

# Pentecost 1

Thomas G. Long

## Series A

**FORTRESS PRESS**          **MINNEAPOLIS**

PROCLAMATION 4
Aids for Interpreting the Lessons of the Church Year
Series A: Pentecost 1

Library of Congress Cataloging-in-Publication Data
(Revised for vol. 5–7, ser. A)

Proclamation 4.

Consists of 24 volumes in 3 series designated A, B,
and C, which correspond to the cycles of the three year
lectionary. Each series contains 8 basic volumes with
the following titles: [1] Advent-Christmas, [2] Epiphany,
[3] Lent, [4] Holy Week, [5] Easter, [6] Pentecost 1,
[7] Pentecost 2, and [8] Pentecost 3. In addition there
are four volumes on the lesser festivals.
   By Christopher R. Seitz and others.
   Includes bibliographies.
   1. Bible—Liturgical lessons, English.   2. Bible—
Homiletical use.   3. Bible—Criticism, interpretation, etc.
4. Common lectionary.   5. Church year.
I. Seitz, Christopher R.   II. Proclamation four.
BS391.2.S37   1989      264′.34      88-10982
ISBN 0-8006-4166-3 (Series A, Pentecost 1)

The paper used in this publication meets the minimum requirements of American National Standard for Information Sciences—Permanence of Paper for Printed Library Materials, ANSI Z329.48-1984.                                                                          ∞ ™

Manufactured in the U.S.A.                                                             AF 1–4166

93      92      91      90      89      1      2      3      4      5      6      7      8      9      10

# Contents

The Day of Pentecost                                              5

The Holy Trinity
   The First Sunday after Pentecost                 10

The Second Sunday after Pentecost                                16

The Third Sunday after Pentecost                                 22

The Fourth Sunday after Pentecost                                28

The Fifth Sunday after Pentecost                                 34

The Sixth Sunday after Pentecost                                 40

The Seventh Sunday after Pentecost                               47

The Eighth Sunday after Pentecost                                52

The Ninth Sunday after Pentecost                                 58

Notes                                                            64

# The Day of Pentecost

| Lutheran | Roman Catholic | Episcopal | Common Lectionary |
|---|---|---|---|
| Joel 2:28–29 | Acts 2:1–11 | Acts 2:1–11 | Acts 2:1–21 or Isa. 44:1–8 |
| Acts 2:1–21 | 1 Cor. 12:3b–7, 12–13 | 1 Cor. 12:4–13 | 1 Cor. 12:3b–13 or Acts 2:1–21 |
| John 20:19–23 | John 20:19–23 | John 20:19–23 | John 20:19–23 or John 7:37–39 |

## FIRST LESSON: ACTS 2:1-21

The day of Pentecost is intended to warm the spirit of the church, but at first reading, this Pentecost text will chill the blood of any preacher. The task of preaching, of course, is to extend the life of the biblical text into the present circumstances of the congregation, but, goodness knows, what sermon can possibly come up to the drama of this passage? Here we have a freight train-sized sound of wind from heaven, tongues of fire dancing on the heads of the disciples, United Nations-styled multiple language proclamation, cries of amazement mingled with yelps of mockery among the hearers, and a powerful sermon by Peter that resulted in three thousand baptisms (2:41). This is a Mt. Everest of texts, and we preachers are called to scale it in the midst of congregational worship where the loudest sound heard is the organ, only the candles are on fire, no one cries or yelps save infants, the last baptism was sometime back in February, and the most dramatic movement is the ushers bringing forward the offering plates.

Intimidated preachers would do well, however, to remember the story of Elijah in the cave (1 Kings 19:9-18). There, too, was a strong and rushing wind, and there, too, were great shakings and fire, but the word of God was not in the wind, the earthquake, or the fire, but in the still, small voice . . . the voice.

At Pentecost, too, the word of God is in the voice. The miracle of Pentecost is not that the church received heavenly fireworks; the miracle of Pentecost is that the church was given a voice. "In the last days," says Peter, quoting the prophet Joel, ". . . your sons and daughters shall prophesy" (v. 17). At Pentecost the church did not "find its voice"; it was, rather, gifted with a voice by the Spirit, given something to say and the power to say it, a message of universal scope (vv. 8-10) that would be a blessing to all nations (v. 21).

We can discern this emphasis on proclamation in the symmetry between this account of Pentecost, which serves as a paradigmatic introduction to the whole of Acts, and the story of Jesus' sermon in the synagogue at Nazareth (Luke 4:16-30), which serves as the "master" text for the Gospel of Luke. In both passages a sermon is preached involving an Old Testament prophetic text about the Spirit, and the basic thrust of both sermons is, "Today this scripture has been fulfilled in your hearing." Jesus' sermon cites Isaiah's word, "The Spirit of the Lord is upon me, because he has anointed me to preach good news to the poor . . . to set at liberty those who are oppressed." Jesus' ministry, in other words, is preaching and acts of liberation. Peter's sermon quotes Joel, "I will pour out my Spirit upon all flesh . . . and they shall prophesy. And I will show wonders in the heaven above and signs on the earth beneath." So the church's ministry, like that of Jesus, is one of preaching and signs of God's saving and liberating action.

This voice given to the church is not merely a clergy voice or a stained-glass voice. Indeed, one of the emphases of this Pentecost story is that the church receives its voice in a public place, a place where the whole city could see and hear what was happening (vv. 5-6). Read ahead in Acts, and you will see how many different ways and in how many different places this new voice finds expression. It can be heard, of course, in worship and in Christian education (2:42), but it can also be heard giving comfort to those who are sick (3:6), offering meaning to those who are searching (8:35), announcing healing in places of racial tension (10:34), praying for those in prison (12:5), confronting the exploitation of human beings for profit (16:18), and offering grace even to those who seek to silence it (26:29).

Moreover, the voice given to the church is, intriguingly, a universal voice with a local accent. The crowds can tell that the speakers are Galilean (v. 7), but they are amazed by the fact that all hear in their own native languages (v. 8). The gospel does not abolish local cultures and customs in favor of some vague, one-size-fits-all message that floats above the real lives of people in this place at this time. The gospel is always articulated with some kind of regional accent, in somebody's native tongue. Moving spirituals and lilting plainsong, gospel rock and chanted liturgy, metrical psalms and Salvation Army brass carols—these and others are the local accents of the gospel, the native tongues of those who sing, pray, and preach the gospel. And yet they all point beyond themselves, beyond their regional rhythms, provincial customs, and national vocabularies to the Lord whose salvation fills the whole earth like the waters of the sea (2:21).

An attractive option for preaching on the day of Pentecost is to preach on Joel 2:28-29, the text that stands in the background of the Acts passage.

What makes this text appealing is precisely the fact that in Joel's day, and in ours as well, the text comes as unfulfilled promise. It must surely have astounded Joel's hearers to learn that the choice prophetic gifts of prophesies, dreams, and visions would fall upon such unlikely recipients as daughters, the aged, youth, and servants. Everybody expects prophets, those special representatives of God, to be full of wisdom and visions, but who would ever think that people on Social Security, junior high school students, and motel maids would ever have any word from God to proclaim? But now we learn that God intends to grant these gifts to everyone, even those (perhaps especially those) on the margins of church and society. In Acts we see a *glimpse* of how this promise will be fulfilled, but much remains to be accomplished.

The text, therefore, provides not only a promise of what will be, but also *agenda* for the work of the church, tasks yet to be done. The church must be willing to listen to the aged, to women, to youth, and to those who have no social status. Indeed, the church must be willing to find ways for such people to find their voices. The stakes are high. The issue is not simply charity, but revelation. Our daughters, the aged, youth, and the lowliest of society are not merely the ones who need our care; they are also the ones upon whom God pours the Holy Spirit and who speak God's message for our day.

## EPISTLE: 1 CORINTHIANS 12:3b-13

Services of worship in the church in Corinth must have been something to behold! Just reading between the lines in Paul's letters to them, one gets the picture of a congregation hot-wired into the Spirit. Testimony and prophecy, miracles and tongue-speaking, hymns and revelations—all these and more were standard Lord's Day fare (see 1 Corinthians 14). The place evidently jumped with so much energy and electric excitement that visitors were set to wondering if they had wandered into an asylum rather than a sanctuary (14:23).

The leaders at Corinth had finally concluded that high voltage meant not only "power" but also "danger." Manifestations of the Spirit were heating up worship, but they were also threatening to burn down the church, so they wrote to Paul asking for pastoral advice: What should we do about "spiritual gifts" (12:1)?

Paul recognized that spiritual gifts posed two quite different threats to the Corinthian church: the tendency to chaos and the pressure to conform. On the one hand, all of these volcanic eruptions of the Holy Spirit engendered a very unholy spirit of competition among the members. "My gift is better than yours—or if not better, at least louder." The Corinthians were shouting each other down, and Paul steps in like a kindergarten teacher, saying, "Take turns" (14:27). The Spirit is not a babbler, but a choirmaster, blending the voices of the church into a harmonious chorus. "God is not a God of confusion but of peace" (14:33), so worship should be done "decently and in order" (14:40).

On the other hand, chaotic confusion was not the first danger that Paul identified. To be sure, he urges the Corinthians toward a more orderly style of worship, but before he does that he confronts another, and probably more hazardous, peril: conformity. One solution for the problem at Corinth would have been simply to pull the plug on all of these spiritual gifts. They could have printed a bulletin, arranged the chairs in straight rows, put a team of ushers in place, and eliminated all unpredictability and variety from worship. If anyone dared to exclaim "Jesus is Lord!" during the sermon, that person could have been quietly but firmly escorted to the narthex to cool off.

Paul, however, took another view. "No one can say 'Jesus is Lord,' " he insisted, "except by the Holy Spirit" (v. 3b). And what is more, he maintained, all of these bursting expressions of the faith—revelations, healings, miracles, prophecies, tongues, interpretations—*all* of them are the gifts of the one Spirit of God in Christ (v. 11). At this point in his letter, Paul is not arguing "*e pluribus unum*" ("From the many, one"), but precisely the opposite: From the one Spirit come *many* gifts, and all of this variety is provided for the benefit of the whole church (v. 7).

Every congregation lives, of course, with some of the tension felt at Corinth. There are people lobbying for greater social involvement, and people lobbying for a deeper spirituality. There are teachers and preachers, givers of blessings and workers of mighty deeds. There are singers and pray-ers, and there are silent servants of mercy. There are prophets and program leaders, people with brilliant insight and people who simply know how to love others. Inevitably such variety creates some degree of confusion, and even competition, in the life of the church. Every congregation must somehow harness this energy into a peaceful and unified church life. Paul reminds us, however, that if this peace and unity come at the expense of the celebration of the Spirit's astounding diversity, then the price has been too high.

## GOSPEL: JOHN 20:19-23

It's a story-telling technique Hollywood has learned well. A movie opens with a series of seemingly random and disconnected scenes. This happens, now that happens, then something else happens, but nothing connects, nothing fits together. In the darkened theater hands pause hesitantly over boxes of buttery popcorn and brows knit with perplexity. What's going on here? What is this *about*? Then, suddenly, the key appears, and everything falls into place. Aha! So that's it! He's really a double agent, or she's planning a jewel heist. Jagged pieces of the plot quickly fit together into a pattern of meaning.

Just so, there is simply no way to make this story in John flow smoothly and logically. This happens and that happens, but none of it seems to connect. It is the first day of the week, and the disciples are locked away in a room somewhere "for fear of the Jews." Suddenly Jesus is standing among them saying "Shalom—Peace be with you." (How did he get in? Did he pass through the locked door? Why, of all the things he might have said, does he say "Shalom"? John offers no comment.) Then Jesus shows them his hands and side (what prompted that?), and the disciples are said to be glad to see him (a curious reaction to a display of wounds). Jesus responds by saying (again?), "Peace be with you." Then comes another seeming non sequitur, "As the Father has sent me, even so I send you." It's hard to say what we expect next, but surely not what happens, namely, that Jesus breathes on them and makes a pronouncement about receiving the Holy Spirit and forgiving and retaining sins. What's going on here? What is this *about*?

At this point the modern reader may still have a brow knitted with puzzlement, but the first readers of John's Gospel were already sending up cheers of recognition. The story is full of images from and allusions to the worship of the Johannine community, and the text practically shouts at the original readers, "Don't read this as straight narration; read this *liturgically*; hear this through the ears of your community worship." Once the liturgical key is introduced, once the template of Sunday worship is placed over the story, the apparently disjointed events fall into place. John's church worshiped "on the first day of the week," perhaps in "the evening" and surely in the context of conflict with and "fear of" the Jewish synagogue. "Peace be with you" and "Even so I send you" are liturgical formulae, and Baptism and the Eucharist are echoed in the breathing of the Holy Spirit, the word about forgiveness of sins, and the showing of the physical wounds of Christ. In sum, this story is not only a description of what happened with the disciples that first Easter, but also an affirmation of what happens every Lord's Day when the followers of Christ gather for worship.

Christians no longer worship behind locked doors "for fear of the Jews" (sadly, in some places it is more likely that synagogues would lock their doors "for fear of the Christians"), but it is true that Christian worship still takes place in the midst of a world of violence and opposition. Medieval cathedrals were often decorated with the faces of gargoyles and demons to remind the church of the darkness that ever surrounds the gospel's circle of light. Despite easy talk of a "Christian society," the fact is that the truth of the gospel threatens the powers-that-be to their core. Christians need only to look at the experience of the church in South Africa to be reminded that the world will do its best to domesticate the true witness to Christ and, failing that, to destroy it.

The temptation is to file the demanding edges off of the gospel, to somehow make it more socially acceptable and less risky, or to lock the doors, dim the lights, and hope that the world will forget where we are hidden. Instead, the risen Christ comes to us as we worship, not with condemnation, but with a word of *shalom* that both meets and transforms our fears. "Peace I leave with you," he promised. "My peace I give to you; not as the world gives do I give to you. Let not your hearts be troubled, neither let them be afraid" (14:27). Equipped with Christ's peace, and in the power of the Spirit, we are once again freed from the fear of the world, and also freed to unlock the church doors and bear witness in the world. "As the Father has sent me, even so I send you."

# The Holy Trinity
# The First Sunday after Pentecost

| Lutheran | Roman Catholic | Episcopal | Common Lectionary |
|---|---|---|---|
| Gen. 1:1—2:3 | Exod. 34:4b–6, 8–9 | Gen. 1:1—2:3 | Deut. 4:32–40 |
| 2 Cor. 13:11–14 | 2 Cor. 13:11–13 | 2 Cor. 13:11–14 | 2 Cor. 13:5–14 |
| Matt. 28:16–20 | John 3:16–18 | Matt. 28:16–20 | Matt. 28:16–20 |

## FIRST LESSON: GENESIS 1:1—2:3

Many modern people carry around in their heads two views of the beginning of the cosmos: a "scientific" view and the "Genesis" view that "in the beginning God created the heavens and the earth" (1:1). Except for a few stubborn creationists, most people of faith are content to let these two views coexist in a mutual, if uneasy, alliance. The "scientific" view (whether it be the "Big Bang" theory or something else) tells us the facts about *how* the universe came to be; Genesis tells us *who* brought it into being. The former is a matter of physics; the latter is a conviction of theology; and that's that.

While it is certainly true that the Genesis account of creation should not be turned into biology and astrophysics (and all of the insistent attempts to do so are pseudoscience at best), it does make more radical claims upon us than merely "whatever happened at the beginning of time, God was in there somewhere." Indeed, we have become so accustomed to the familiar words of this text that we have lost sight of the truth that this magnificent hymn was crafted not only to proclaim that God created the cosmos, but also as a protest *against* certain rival understandings of what it means to live as human beings out there in the world. The Hebrews ran into those alternative views in Babylon during the exile, the period during which this text received its definitive form, but some of these understandings persist in modern garb, and the text continues to protest against them.

First, there is the notion of sheer, unbridled *chaos* as the basic force of the universe, that the universe is a product of random and capricious energies, whirling meaninglessly and wildly out of control. "The stars blindly run," and life doesn't grow; it just spreads, like cancer. Tragedy strikes, and we can only shrug, "Well, that's the way things are." There is no history in the meaningful sense, only "one damned thing after another." Over against this the text announces that we live not in chaos, but in *creation*. God's creative activity is always at work, turning the formless, chaotic void (1:2) into the ordered and meaningful good (see Romans 8:28). Again and again God creates by speaking a word, calling forth light and placing the chaotic darkness under discipline (1:35), summoning forth the dry land and subduing the restless and terrible energies of the sea (9:9-10). Over a dozen times in the text God *speaks*, driving home the truth that we live not in an "uncalled for" world of disorder, but in a universe that has been divinely "called for."

Next, there is the view that the world and human life are the product of *fate*, disinterested and distant gods, unseen and unconcerned forces. "God does not play dice with the universe," Einstein is reported to have said, and indeed, the picture in the text is of God purposefully at work in the making of all things, joyfully forming the creation, delighting in all that is made, blessing the human creatures and giving gifts to them, calling all of creation "good," and resting in contentment when the work of creation is done.

Finally, there is the view that *creation is God*, that the divine energy has been fully absorbed into the world. In this text God is intimately involved in the creation of the cosmos, but God is also separate from the created order. Do not bow down before mountains and sunsets, beautiful though they may be, for nature is not God. Fold up the astrological charts, for the divine is not to be identified with the heavenly bodies. Step down from our arrogant thrones of domination, for even human beings, the crown of creation, are not God. Ultimate meaning cannot be manufactured out of the things at hand, but can only be found in communion with God who speaks the inviting and blessing to the human creatures and who "in the beginning created the heavens and the earth."

## ALTERNATIVE FIRST LESSON: DEUTERONOMY 4:32-40

How is it that people get motivated to perform their responsibilities? A worker slacks off on the job; a student stops studying; an elected official grows deaf to the needs of the citizens; a company ignores the consumer. How can a fire be lit under such people to encourage them to do what they are supposed to do? One way, of course, is to threaten them. Tell them that they will be fired, be flunked, be voted out of office, go bankrupt, or be taken to court. Let them know that if their behavior does not change for the better, there will be dire consequences. But is this the most effective way?

The editor of Deuteronomy faced just such a motivational challenge. The book was addressed to Israel during a time, probably in the 8th century B.C., when their faithfulness to the commandments of God was at a low ebb. The gods of culture were worshiped; the society was socially unjust; and the ancient law of God was gathering dust in empty sanctuaries. So the writer or writers of Deuteronomy summoned the figure of Moses to their pages to give a long motivational sermon, calling Israel back to its responsibilities as the people of God. There are, to be sure, threats of dire consequences. If the people worship idols, Moses warns, then "I call heaven and earth to witness against you this day, that you will soon utterly perish from the land . . ." (4:26).

It is crucial to see, however, that threat is not the only word, or finally the enduring word in Deuteronomy, and today's text speaks another word beyond threat. People can be motivated to renew their responsibilities not only by hanging the prospect of punishment over their heads, but also by refreshing the vision of what caused them to take on those responsibilities in the first place. People can be revived not only by warning them of the terrible things that could happen, but also by reminding them of *who* they truly are. Indeed, in this passage, Moses rehearses Israel's past, recalling what kind of people they are and what sort of God brought them into being.

No greater event has occurred in history, Moses claims, than the birth of Israel as the special people of God. What other nation has heard the voice of God speaking out of the burning bush? What other nation has been so mightily delivered from slavery? What other nation has been so firmly and lovingly led, been so graciously given a land, as Israel (vv. 33-39)? Only after Moses has reminded Israel of the gracious deeds and the lovingkindness of God, only when Moses has shown around the baby pictures and the family album of the cherished people called Israel, only then do the "therefores" of this text come. "Therefore . . . know that the Lord is God. Therefore . . . you shall keep God's commandments . . ." (vv. 39-40).

One is reminded of Luther's word to himself in times of crisis and doubt: "I am baptized." Sometimes when people of faith remember who they are, they gain new insight and commitment about what they are to do as God's chosen ones.

### EPISTLE: 2 CORINTHIANS 13:5-14

The situation is this: Some harsh critics in the Corinthian congregation have challenged the authority and integrity of Paul. The Corinthian congregation had been founded by Paul, and Paul was their spiritual mentor, but now a contentious group has accused him, among other things, of being weak (10:10), deceitful and crafty (12:16), and a miserable speaker (11:6). Their charges have called his apostolic status onto the carpet, have portrayed him as a greedy shyster, and have insinuated that he is incompetent. In short, they have put his entire ministry to the test.

Paul had already planned to make a visit, his third (12:14; 13:1), to the Corinthians, but now that these critics have been taking target practice with his reputation, Paul fears that his trip may turn from a joyous reunion to a bitter wrangle (12:20-21). In an attempt to clear the air before he arrives on their doorstep, Paul writes a letter to Corinth. Some scholars think that 2 Corinthians 10-13 was originally a separate letter sent by Paul to defend his standing as an apostle and to pave the way for a constructive visit. In any case, 13:5-14 clearly has this upcoming encounter with the Corinthian congregation in view, and in his passage Paul basically advances the following proposal: You Corinthians have put me to the test; I suggest that you put yourselves to a test.

"Test yourselves," Paul urges them, "to see whether you are holding to your faith" (v. 5). Indeed, if the Corinthians can pass this test, Paul argues, then he, too, will have received a passing grade in his own test (v. 6), because the truest measure of his ministry is whether it has enabled the Corinthians to be strong in their faith (vv. 8-9). Paul is making a very clever case here. The Lord has given him authority, he claims, "for building up and not for tearing down" (v. 10). He preached the gospel to the Corinthians, so if they have been "built up" in the faith, their very strength demonstrates his divine authority.

Two major emphases appear in this text, and the preacher may choose to employ either or both in the sermon. First there is the idea that the true measure of any Christian ministry or service is to be found not in the achievements of those who perform it, but in what it means to those who receive it. This does not imply, of course, that all authentic ministry is "successful" in the conventional sense of that term; it means rather that all authentic ministry is "other-directed." Christian faith seeks to serve others, and the real test of its authority lies in how much others are built up, not how much those who minister are built up. As long as the Corinthians hold on to their faith, Paul is content to be the broken apostle, wounded leader, and halting speaker. Indeed, God's "power is made perfect in weakness" (12:9), and "we are glad when we are weak and you (in Corinth) are strong" (v. 9).

The other major emphasis in the passage falls upon the Corinthians themselves. They want to test the validity of the church by measuring the eloquence of their ministers, the virtue of their officers, and the charm of their teachers. They want their programs sound, their budget dollars accounted for, their youth ministry vigorous, their church school rooms color-coordinated, and their preachers polished. Paul reminds them, however, that faith grows best in the soil of weakness. In the midst of conflict, and pain, and inarticulate apostles bearing stammering witness to the gospel, God has given them "signs and wonders and mighty works" (12:12). The yardstick for the Christian church is not the well-rounded program and the well-turned pulpit phrase, but "Jesus Christ in you" (v. 5).

## GOSPEL: MATTHEW 28:16-20

Beware! Matthew has built this text with linguistic trapdoors, mirrored walls, and secret passageways that lead to earlier references in his Gospel. Preachers should read this passage aloud to themselves very carefully and slowly, pausing to ponder over the multiple levels at play in each phrase.

Take the opening line, for example: "Now the eleven disciples went to Galilee . . ." (v. 16). Instinctively, we want to read "the *twelve* disciples." Throughout his Gospel, Matthew has used the term "the twelve" so frequently that it has become a catch phrase. It rolls off our lips as effortlessly as "the seven seas" or "the four winds," but now we stumble over the new formulation: "the *eleven* disciples." Matthew has placed the memory of Judas's betrayal and the sudden awareness of broken community as stumbling blocks in the reader's path.

The eleven go, Matthew tells us, "to the mountain to which Jesus had directed them." But once again the reader stumbles: Which mountain was that? Jesus said nothing in his instructions to the women about a specific mountain (v. 10). Indeed, we will not find this mountain on a map of Galilee, but rather on the theological map of Matthew's Gospel. The mountain where Jesus delivered the Sermon on the Mount (5:1), the mountain where Jesus fed the crowds (15:29), the mountain where Jesus was transfigured (17:1), and this mountain (v. 16) merge into a unified theological symbol: the place of revelation. The disciples, then, go to an unspecified geographical location in Galilee; the reader is invited to travel with them to the explicit place of revelation. The disciples go because of a demand placed upon them ("Go to Galilee . . ."); the reader follows in the hope that something also will be given to them.

Matthew encourages us with the news that, when the disciples saw the risen Christ, "they worshiped him" (v. 17). Yet even as we settle into our satisfaction over learning this, a trapdoor opens in the sentence, and the reader falls through to the disheartening counterword that "some doubted." For their part, the women "took hold of Jesus' feet and worshiped him" (v. 9), but not so the disciples. Even the sight of the risen Jesus cannot filter the pollution of doubt from their worship.

It is now, and only now, that we are truly prepared to hear the words of the risen Christ, the promise and the command that end Matthew's Gospel. If Matthew had not caused us to stumble and falter, we could easily mistake Christ's word as a chipper, triumphalistic, church growth slogan. Mobilize the resources of the church! Form the mission task forces! Unfurl the banners! "Into All The World, Making Disciples!" "Like a Mighty Army, Moves the Church of God!" But the reader now knows better. We are painfully aware that the church, embodied in these disciples, possesses no resources to mobilize, has no troop strength to send into the fray. No number of confident slogans, bold buildings, hefty budgets, or mission strategies can mask the fact that, by itself, the church has nothing of what it takes to perform Christ's mission.

We hear, then, the irony of Christ's words. It is to a diminished and broken community of disciples, to the ones whose "church growth statistics" have gone from twelve to eleven, that he says, "Make disciples of all nations." It is to those whose worship is pervaded by doubt that he gives the charge to baptize. It is the very ones who "forsook him and fled" (26:56) that he now calls to teach the nations to observe all his commandments. Where will they get the strength for this? They have nothing.

"All authority in heaven and on earth has been given to me," Jesus told them. "And, lo I am with you always, to the close of the age" (vss. 18, 20). In this promise, the church, having nothing, is given everything.

# The Second Sunday after Pentecost

| Lutheran | Roman Catholic | Episcopal | Common Lectionary |
|---|---|---|---|
| Deut. 11:18–21, 26–28 | Deut. 11:18, 26–28, 32 | Deut. 11:18–21, 26–28 | Gen. 12:1–9 |
| Rom. 3:21–25a, 27–28 | Rom. 3:21–25a, 28 | Rom. 3:21–25a, 28 | Rom. 3:21–28 |
| Matt. 7:21–29 | Matt. 7:21–27 | Matt. 7:21–27 | Matt. 7:21–29 |

## FIRST LESSON: DEUTERONOMY 11:18-21, 26-28

The major portion of the Book of Deuteronomy consists of a lengthy exhortation given by Moses to the people of Israel just as they are about to move from the wilderness into the promised land. Most scholars are persuaded, however, that Deuteronomy was written much later, probably around the 8th century B.C., as a response to the social crisis of that period. The nation had become religiously confused, with sanctuaries all over the land mixing and matching elements of Canaanite religion with the worship of Yahweh. Moreover, influential people in the land were more concerned about garnering personal wealth and securing the national defense than they were about such matters as the plight of the poor, zeal for righteousness, or the fact that bribing judges had become an everyday scandal. In the midst of this mess Deuteronomy appeared, thus enabling the voice of Moses himself to confront the crisis and to remind the nation of the covenant with God that gave them birth as a people. In other words, Deuteronomy provides a dramatic rendering of the past in order to correct the corruption of the present.

It is not difficult, of course, to draw the linkages between the social situation of Deuteronomy and our own time of corporate greed, leveraged buyouts, military madness, loss of religious focus, and widespread poverty and homelessness. What the preacher should avoid, however, is making a simplistic leap to the conclusion that the text's solution to what ails our society is to be found in some righteous return to an earlier period in our history. Returning to a purer, simpler time (if there ever was one) is not an option for our culture, nor was it an option for the first readers of Deuteronomy either. No society can ever fully reconstruct what used to be in a time gone by.

Deuteronomy, in fact, does not call for this. It is not a "back to the Bible," "back to the farm," "back to the nuclear family" document. Rather, it employs a portrayal of national history as a means to remind the people of those enduring qualities that, in all times and circumstances, enable a society to be just, faithful, and human. The goal of Deuteronomy is not nostalgia for an idealized past, but reform toward an obedient future.

The first portion of the text (vv. 18-21) calls for the people to "lay up these words of mine in your heart and in your soul." "These words" refers to all of the sayings of the book, especially the commands to love and serve the Lord with earnestness, to abandon the worship of all other gods, to live together justly, and to have compassion on the homeless, the poor, and the stranger (see 10:12-22). These commandments are not to become ceremonies observed only in chapels and muttered ritualistically on holidays; they are to be the constant bread and drink, the air and water of the people. For Deuteronomy, "Glory to God in the highest" is not a motto for a Christmas card, but the central truth of human life, worthy to be taught and discussed daily (v. 19), and "execute justice" is not a once-a-year charity campaign, but a way of being in the world (vv. 20-21).

The second part of the text (vv. 26-28) points to the urgency of obeying God's commandments. The language is of "blessing and curse," and the point is not that God will "get them" if they are bad. The point is that God tells the truth about what makes for fully human life, and to live any other way is to live a lie. In Anne Tyler's novel *Dinner at the Homesick Restaurant*, an elementary school child asks his mother one day, "Mother, if it turned out that money grew on trees, just for one day and never again, would you let me stay home from school to pick it?" His mother tells him that she would not. He is puzzled and wonders why she would refuse to let him take advantage of this one-day spree. She says that his education is more important. "Other kids' mothers would let them, I bet," the child counters. "Other mothers don't have plans for their children to amount to something," she replies.[1] The commandments of God are gifts from a Parent who wants us to amount to something. They are not the trival demands of a fussy teacher. ("Write your name on the *top* of the paper, not the bottom. Write only on one side of the paper.") They are the secrets about what makes life human: love of God and neighbor. We weren't made for the sake of the commandments; the commandments were made for us (see Mark 2:27).

## ALTERNATIVE FIRST LESSON: GENESIS 12:1-9

Genesis 12:1 constitutes one of the major turning points in the biblical story. At this point, the narrative moves from the history of humanity in general to the peculiar history of Israel, from the broad account of the people God *created* to the special recital of the people God *calls*, from the report of the curse to the adventure of the renewed blessing. As such, this passage can only be understood against the backdrop of all that has been told before, as a new beginning and a fresh word set over against the old circumstances of Genesis 1–11.

The text begins with, "Now the Lord said . . ." (v. 1), and we hear in those words an echo of much that has gone before in Genesis. Once again we have the familiar action of the speech of God. The Lord, who commanded light out of darkness, dry land out of the chaos of the seas, the creation of humankind in God's own image, redemption through Noah in a time of wickedness, now speaks again to create and to redeem.

God speaks to Abram both a *command* and a *promise*. The *command* is to "go," to leave behind all that has defined Abram's past. Notice how radical this command is for Abram. In the ancient world, one's total identity could be defined by three principal relationships. First, and most important, a person belonged to an immediate family, to one's own household. Then came one's clan, one's larger set of family and kin. Finally, there was one's tribe, one's nation. Abram is commanded to leave all three behind, and the command comes in three stages, each stripping away a set of relationships more intimate than the one before: Leave your country . . . leave your kindred . . . leave your father's house (v. 1).

The *promise* hearkens back both to the curses of Eden (Genesis 3) and to the vanity of Babel (Genesis 11). Humanity, once banished from the garden and burdened with the toilsome tilling of the earth, is now, in Abram, promised a new land (v. 1). Humanity, once weighed down with painful childbirth, is now promised, in Abram, the parentage of a great nation (v. 2). Humanity, which arrogantly attempted to build a tower to heaven and to make for itself a great name, is now promised, in Abram, the very greatness they could not grasp by their own might (v. 2). Humanity, once cursed, is now promised, in Abram, a great blessing (vv. 2-3).

And how does Abram respond? "So Abram went as the Lord told him" (v. 4). Abram obeyed the command and believed the promise, and in so doing, became a model for faith thereafter (see Romans 4; Hebrews 11:8-12). Two other aspects of this passage underscore its power as a description not only of Abram's faith, but also of the experience of all faithful people. First, when Abram gets to the land of promise, he finds Canaanites already living there (v. 6), and he sets up altars to God near Canaanite settlements (vv. 7-8). In other words, like Abram, faithful people are always in the position of worshiping and obeying God and celebrating the promises of God in the midst of other people in the land who do not heed the commands and do not believe the promises. The first readers of this text would have certainly recognized that they, as Abram's descendants, had often found these Canaanites, their customs and their religion, seductive and more attractive than the promises of God. Second, the author of this text is surprisingly silent about Abram's destination. The reader is told much about Abram's journey, but his final destination is not named here. The passage ends by not ending, by saying "and Abram journeyed on, still going . . ." (v. 9). The early Christians, who were sometimes called the People of the Way (Acts 9:2; 24:14,22), would surely have known how it is that God calls faithful people to be those who "journey on, still going. . . ."

## EPISTLE: ROMANS 3:21-28

Reading through this passage carefully will quickly determine its theological center of gravity: the righteousness of God. In these few verses, the theme of God's righteousness is named no fewer than four times (vv. 21, 22, 25, 26); it throbs like a drumbeat throughout the text. So what? The thought that God is righteous is a nice idea, as far as theological ideas go. It is far more comforting, for instance, than the notion that God is a bully and a malicious outlaw, but what real difference does it make to contemporary people that there is a God out there somewhere who fortunately happens to be righteous? Theological concepts, if they are to have value, must be grounded somewhere in human experience.

The theological claim that God is righteous has, as a matter of fact, much to do with human experience. Basic human questions, such as "Does life have any meaning?" "Is it possible to live in freedom?" and "Does it make any enduring difference how we treat each other?" find their answers, Paul maintains, in a deeper and more basic question about the character of God, who stands at the center of life. If the God who created the world and human life is full of caprice and whim, then creation is a cruel joke and life is "a tale told by an idiot." The human search for ultimate meaning becomes a wild-goose chase, since there is no ultimate meaning to be found, and the concern for ethics reduces to "you only go 'round once in life, so grab all the gusto you can get."

But God is not capricious and arbitrary. God's integrity and trustworthiness hold creation together, which is another way of saying that the righteousness of God is revealed in creation and that life discloses ultimate meaning at its core. All people everywhere know this, Paul maintains, since God "has been clearly perceived in the things that have been made" (1:20). It is as if the music of God's faithfulness reverberates through the whole of creation, and what it means to be fully human—free, purposeful, and in community—is to resonate with this life-giving music. Even so, the human condition turned sour; people worshiped the creation instead of the creator, tried to forge their own meaning and freedom by composing other, and finally discordant, songs. Thus, humanity exchanged the truth for a lie (1:25).

So God again revealed the divine integrity, this time to the Jews in the law, but humanity, trapped in the downward spiral of sin, could not dance to that melody any better than they could to the divine harmony in creation. If people could obey the law, life would be restored to its true meaning, but they could not. The law, then, did not put life back in tune; in the face of human rebellion, it only disclosed the depth of human failure (3:20).

"But now. . . . but now. . . ." That is how Paul begins this passage (v. 21). Something new has stirred; the curtain has been pulled back to disclose yet another divine initiative to set people free. "But now the righteousness of God has been manifested . . . through faith in Jesus Christ" (vv. 21-22). Lost humanity could not find its way home; lost humanity built its search for meaning around a lie; lost humanity broke harmony with God, with nature, and with itself. Humanity is without excuse (2:1) and God has every reason to say, in the deepest theological sense, "to hell with it." But now . . . another word is spoken; but now . . . humanity is restored by God's "grace as a gift" (v. 24). Through the sacrifice of Jesus, God put an end to the brokenness of human life (v. 25).

So what does it mean to be fully human? It means to trust, to have faith, that at the center of life there is a divine giver of great gifts. Indeed, *that* is what "the righteousness of God" has meant all along. The picture is not of a prim, neatly pressed, upright schoolmaster deity who compromises the divine rectitude for a moment in order to give these naughty human students yet another chance. The picture is of a passionate, loving God who will not let us go. Giving, saving, and forgiving *are* the expressions of this loving God's righteousness (v. 25). The God who gave the moon, the sun, and the stars; the God who breathed life into humanity; the God who gave the liberating Law—this God now freely gives justification through Jesus Christ. To be human is to have faith that this is so and to build one's life in trust around the gracious righteousness of this God whose very purpose is to give us good gifts (vv. 27-28).

## GOSPEL: MATTHEW 7:21-29

In his book describing his career as a psychotherapist, F. Robert Rodman begins with these words: "Every patient stared at long enough, listened to hard enough, yields up a child . . . caught up in a confused life, trying to do the right thing, whatever that may be, and doing the wrong thing instead."[2]

Trying to do the right thing, and doing the wrong thing instead—this is the concern at the heart of this passage from Matthew. Commentators agree that the language of this text has been firmly shaped by the situation in Matthew's own church, and that situation is that there are plenty of folk who mean well but who miss the kingdom nevertheless. Some of them have their liturgical act together, and at just the proper moment in the service, and with all the correct feeling, they cry, *"Kyrie, Kyrie"* ("Lord, Lord"). Others in Matthew's congregation are heavily invested in the dramatic forms of the church's ministry. They prophesy enthusiastically, cast out demons energetically, and perform mighty works across the land, and all "in the name of Christ."

And what's wrong with that? Most congregations, of course, would be glad to hear a few more heartfelt "Lord, Lords" in worship, would be heartened by the addition of some "mighty workers" to the rolls, whatever the reasons. Matthew, however, sees the potential for destruction beneath the good intentions of these people, and he turns some of the most frightening of all the words of Jesus on them: "I will declare to them, 'I never knew you; depart from me, you evildoers.' " (v. 23).

This stern reaction is provoked by Matthew's conviction that the true measure of a Christian community is not the beauty of its worship, the achievements of its ministry, or even the sincerity of its belief, but only its obedience to the commandments of its Lord. This text comes at the end of Jesus' Sermon on the Mount, and there the church is commanded to build its life, worship, and ministry on the foundation of mercy, meekness, peacemaking, purity of heart, extravagant forgiveness, radical love of enemies, and the diligent seeking first of God's kingdom and righteousness. Churches can, of course, build upon other foundations, and in the process they may, in fact, look good and mean well. But in doing so, they serve themselves and not Christ, who will ultimately say to them, "I never knew you."

Matthew would be saddened, but not surprised probably, to see some of the church advertisements on the religion page of the newspaper. There congregations present themselves as places of comforting worship ("Hear the choir sing 'Lord, Lord' ") and exciting ministry ("Miracles Every Sunday!", "The Friendly Church Where You Can Find a Home!"). The worship soars, the pews are comfortably full of people trying to do the right thing, the air conditioning hums, the programs spin, but when the rains fall, and the floods wash away the cultural silt, and the winds blow off the ornaments and trappings, the church will stand or fall by virtue of its true foundation. "The last temptation," wrote T. S. Eliot, "is the greatest treason: To do the right deed for the wrong reason."[3] It is the right deed, of course, to cry "Lord, Lord," but, "Not every one who says to me, 'Lord, Lord,' shall enter the kingdom of heaven but the one who does the will of my Father who is in heaven."

# The Third Sunday after Pentecost

| Lutheran | Roman Catholic | Episcopal | Common Lectionary |
|---|---|---|---|
| Hos. 5:15—6:6 | Hos. 6:3–6 | Hos. 5:15—6:6 | Gen. 22:1–18 |
| Rom. 4:18–25 | Rom. 4:18–25 | Rom. 4:13–18 | Rom. 4:13–18 |
| Matt. 9:9–13 | Matt. 9:9–13 | Matt. 9:9–13 | Matt. 9:9–13 |

### FIRST LESSON: HOSEA 5:15—6:6

The book of Hosea is justifiably famous for its rich and provocative images. Hosea is depicted as a man who is told by God to marry a prostitute (1:2-3), and his predictably shaky marriage becomes a metaphor for the relationship between God and Israel. Just as Hosea's wife is adulterous, pursuing other lovers, so Israel is faithless, worshiping other gods and abandoning the way of justice. Or again, God is portrayed as a distraught parent, angered at the child's disobedience, but also remembering that "it was I who taught Ephraim to walk" (11:3), and finally crying out with anguished love, "How can I give you up, O Ephraim!" (12:8).

Among Old Testament scholars, however, the book of Hosea is famous not only for its images, but also for its textual difficulties. The literary style is sometimes episodic and often puzzling. It is not always clear how some sections of the book connect to the surrounding material, and the passage in view is one of these ambiguous texts. A case can be made for at least two quite different interpretations, and the preacher must choose between them. Before we can make that choice, though, we need to understand something of the historical background.

The historical context is almost surely the Syro-Ephramite war of 734 B.C. The Assyrian army mounted a hostile move toward Palestine, and a panicky Israel quickly attempted to forge defense alliances with its neighbors. Judah refused to join, and, like bitter siblings, Israel and Judah engaged in angry border skirmishes. The result was that Judah sneaked over the border and occupied some of Israel's territory.

In the midst of this messy situation Hosea announces God's judgment upon both nations—against Judah for taking advantage of the situation and greedily grabbing more land (5:10) and against Israel for seeking deliverance through political alliances instead of from God (5:13). God intends to have nothing to do with either of these wayward children, Hosea tells them, but instead is leaving the scene until they come to their senses and repent (5:15).

Now comes the difficulty: Do Israel and Judah, faced with this word of judgment, repent, or don't they? The verses that follow (6:1-3) constitute a beautiful, liturgical prayer of repentance, but is this a prayer that Israel and Judah actually utter, or is it a prayer God *hopes* these two faithless nations will someday confess? [The transitional word "saying," which appears at the end of v. 15 in the RSV and would seem to clear up the ambiguity, does not appear in the original Hebrew.]

If it is the latter, then the picture is of a brokenhearted God, lifting the divine hands in exasperation, "What am I going to do with you two? How can I bring you to your knees?" (6:4). God will not let these cherished people go, but disciplines them through the prophetic word of judgment (6:5) toward that day when their love will be more enduring than the morning dew (6:4) and their knowledge of God's saving power deep and steadfast (6:3).

If, however, verses 6:1-3 are a prayer already on the lips of Israel and Judah, then we have a quite different picture. They pray, but their prayer is superficial and born of desperation. Israel and Judah have gotten into trouble and, like many in crisis, they have turned to the formula of prayer as a last resort: "O Lord, get us out of this!" To this God responds with a *critique* of their prayer, "What shall I do with you? Don't give me your ritual prayers; give me steadfast love. Don't murmur your lovely liturgical 'burnt offerings;' bring me your deep and faithful repentance."

Perhaps we finally will not have to choose between these two interpretations, since both are true. Hosea announces to those who trust only in Wall Street, NATO, or the Warsaw Pact, that God's deliberate and judging absence from their lives will, like a vacuum, draw them back toward prayerful obedience. And also for those who mumble, week after week, "Lord have mercy. . . . Come, let us return to the Lord. . . . Get me out of this one, Jesus," but who then leave their pews to live the same faithless lives as before, God will not allow their prayers to remain forever empty. In short, however we translate this text, the picture is the same: Where there used to be a lush garden there is now a vast and vacant lot between our house and God's. It is vacant because some of us no longer go there to prayerfully cultivate it and because others of us have choked out the flowers of righteousness with our weedy neglect of justice and the drought of our half-hearted worship. The good news of this text is that God will not allow that land between us to be spoiled forever, for God's "going forth is as sure as the dawn; God will come to us as the showers, as the spring rains that water the earth" (6:3).

## ALTERNATIVE FIRST LESSON: GENESIS 22:1-18

There is no room in this wild, challenging, and finally beautiful story for the timid or the tidy-minded. This text "says so much and evokes so much," maintains W. Dow Edgerton, "that it threatens to overwhelm us. There are echoes and harmonies, resonances and reverberations, relationships, patterns woven into the surface, and color stained deep into the background. It is all filled with meaning, but what meaning?"[4]

Modern readers are almost inevitably offended by the picture of God in the story. How could God command the death of a human being, a child, a cherished son, even if God never really intended to allow Abraham to go through with the sacrifice? That is an understandable question, but it is question too small for this text, or more precisely, too small for the God disclosed by this text. The God of this story is not the reasonable, well-mannered, domesticated God to whom we can blandly pray, "Help us to be better people," as if *we* are going to use our own resources to be better people anyway but would like a little divine help in the process. The God of this story is the God from whom all things flow, who needs none else; the God above all gods, who tolerates no others, the radical God who has absolute power over life and death and who in utter freedom gives and takes away.

God's command to Abraham begins with three repetitive phrases that underscore the enormity of what is being asked: "Take your *son* . . . your *only son* . . . *Isaac*, whom you love . . . and offer him . . ." (v.2). Isaac is not only the child of Abraham's heart, he is also the child of the promise of God (Gen. 18:1-15). Without Isaac, there is no way for God's promise, that Abraham would be the father of a great nation, to be fulfilled. Dramatically, and ironically, Abraham can obey and trust God only by destroying the very one through whom the trustworthy promise of God was to be established. It was not a dilemma that Abraham could understand or explain; no human being could do that. He could only decide. Could he trust God when all reasonable ground for that trusting was cut away? It was the decision that Jesus faced in Gethsemane; it was the decision the disciples faced standing at the foot of the cross.

In a touching and powerful moment, as Abraham responds to Isaac's puzzlement, he discloses both his own radical faith and the central theological claim of this story: "God will provide himself the lamb for a burnt offering, my son" (v. 8). Abraham does not comprehend this; he confesses it. As Paul said of Abraham, "No distrust made him waver concerning the promise of God" (Rom. 4:20).

And so Abraham picked up the knife and began to move it along its slow, sad, obedient path. But then he hears a voice, and we hear it as well. An angel's voice speaks to Abraham, and to us, the welcome and unexpected good news of deliverance. Then "Abraham lifted up his eyes and looked," the narrator tells us, and we, the readers, look too. "Behold . . . ," says

the narrator, and we strain our eyes to see. "Behold . . . ," we are commanded, and so we look. We see, of course, what Abraham sees, a ram
caught by the horns in a thicket, but we also see the other reality that
Abraham sees: The God from whom all things flow, the God above all
gods, who tolerates no others, the radical God who in utter freedom gives
and takes away, is a God of grace who provides life out of death. "Behold . . . ," we are told, and we peer through the dim and the death into
the promised future of God to see at last "the Lamb of God, who takes
away the sin of the world" (John 1:29).

## EPISTLE: ROMANS 4:13-25

One of the questions that Christians have always had to face is the
relationship between the Christian gospel and the religion of the Old Testament. People from Marcion to the dispensationalists and beyond have
wondered about the apparent discrepancies between the pictures of God
given in the two testaments of the Scripture. Is the Old Testament God,
the God of Abraham and Moses, the God of the law, the same God who
appears in the New Testament, the God of grace who shines forth in the
face of Jesus Christ? If both testaments speak of the same God, then was
the mind of God somehow changed between Old and New? Did God choose
in ancient times to deal with humanity in one manner, portrayed in the
Old Testament, and then decide to change direction and to relate to humanity
in a radically new way in Jesus Christ?

This question was particularly acute for the apostle Paul. Paul and the
earliest Christians had no "New" Testament, of course. The Hebrew Scriptures *were* their Bible. In Romans Paul attempted to describe the essential
character of the gospel, but if it could be shown that his description of the
way God acted in Jesus Christ was radically different from the picture of
God in the Hebrew Scriptures, then his formulation of the gospel would
fall like a house of cards. Throughout the early chapters of Romans, Paul
claimed that the central truth of the gospel is that humanity is justified "by
faith apart from works of law" (3:28). But as soon as those words flowed
out of his pen, he heard his critics (at least in his own mind) objecting,
"Oh yeah? What about Moses? What about Abraham? What about all of
those people in the Hebrew Scriptures? They were called to be holy people,
obedient workers, keepers of the law of God. What is all of this talk about
justification 'apart from works of the law.' Did the mind of God change
all of a sudden, or have you, Paul, misunderstood the whole matter?"

"All right, what about Abraham?" (4:1) asks Paul, never one to run
from a dispute. Forget Moses for the moment; Paul goes right to the
fountainhead of the Old Testament's story of God's making of a people.
Was Abraham righteous? Yes, of course he was, the Scripture says as much

(Gen. 15:6). But was he righteous because he kept the law? No, says Paul, read your Bible more carefully; he was righteous because he "believed God and it was reckoned to him as righteousness." Abraham didn't earn his righteousness, like a wage, by keeping the law; it was given to him as a gift from God. But wait a minute, whispers Paul's inner critic, Abraham was circumcised, wasn't he? That shows that he kept the law. Not so fast, responds Paul, the Scripture calls him "righteous" *before* he was circumcised, not after (4:10).

In our passage Paul continues this dialogical debate, forcefully arguing that "the promise to Abraham . . . did not come through the law but through the righteousness of faith" (4:13). In other words, the whole story of the people of God, including that part of the story told in the Hebrew Scriptures, is the story of a gracious God who makes and keeps promises apart from human merit. Abraham himself did not earn, cause, or create anything. God had promised that Abraham would be "the father of many nations" (v. 17). And what did Abraham bring to this promise? Strength? Hardly, he was nearly a hundred years old and "as good as dead" (v. 19). Great resources? Scarcely, since his wife, Sarah, was as barren as a desert (v. 19). So, what *did* Abraham bring? Faith and hope—that's it. "In hope," Abraham "believed against hope" (v. 18), never wavering in his faith "concerning the promise of God" (v. 20).

God's people, Paul claims, are now and have always been people of faith, people who trust that God keeps promises. By the way, wonders Paul, did Abraham and Sarah ever have any children? Did God really keep that astounding promise? Indeed, God did. In fact, the preacher, standing in the pulpit facing the congregation, is looking at the children of Abraham and Sarah. Abraham and Sarah have many children, since all who trust the promises of God, including the gospel promise that the death and resurrection of Jesus Christ will restore the whole dying creation to life, are the true children of Abraham and Sarah and heirs of the grace of life (vv. 13-14, 23-25).

## GOSPEL: MATTHEW 9:9-13

Do not attempt to clean up the image of the tax agent named Matthew in this passage. Do not think of him as a minor government official with an unfortunate job description, as a troubled businessman with anxious dreams of making his life count, or as an ethical jewel-in-the-rough. Do not romanticize him; do not psychologize him; and do not excuse him. Matthew is a *sinner*, pure and simple. All we are told about him is that he was "sitting at the tax house" (v. 9), but that is enough to know. "Sitting in the tax house" is the New Testament moral equivalent to "shooting up in the heroin alley" or "in the ring of child pornographers." The label "tax collector" is virtually a synonym for greed, graft, collaboration, cultural pollution, and sleaze. Don't try to make it pretty; look at this for what it is. Matthew is a sinner.

Our tendency is not to take it very seriously when the Gospel pictures Matthew the tax collector, or anyone else for that matter, as a sinner. We are so familiar with the Gospel story we have lost the capacity to be shocked by its word about sin. We have heard a thousand times that Jesus is the friend of sinners. And so, when a table full of these characters joins Jesus and the disciples for a meal (9:10), it seems to us as innocent as a family reunion. The Pharisees, everybody's favorite villains, come off, of course, as predictably self-righteous prigs when they dare to ask the disciples, "Why does your teacher eat with tax collectors and sinners?" (v. 11).

What we have done is to allow our easy familiarity with the gospel to blunt its radical claims. In a facile shift of language we automatically think of "sinner" as good and "righteous" as somehow bad, and we plug these reverse definitions into our reading of the New Testament. So, when Jesus tells the Pharisees, "I came not to call the righteous, but sinners" (9:13), we blithely shrug our shoulders and say, "Why, of course."

But if we do that with this passage, which is woven into the intricate fabric of the whole Gospel of Matthew, we are simply not paying attention. "Righteous" is a *good* word in the vocabulary of Matthew's Gospel. In the Gospel of Matthew, it is the righteous who will "shine like the sun in the kingdom" (13:43), and it is the righteous who will enter "into eternal life." People are blessed who "hunger and thirst for righteousness" (5:6) and who "are persecuted for righteousness' sake" (5:10).

So, we misunderstand this passage if we think of it as a multiple-choice test. [Whose side is God on? Choose one: (a) the righteous, or (b) sinners. Why, the correct answer is "b," of course.] The urgent purpose at the heart of this passage is not to get us to decide whether God favors sinners or the righteous; that is a false choice. It is rather to force us to redefine "righteousness," to come to grips with what true righteousness means in the first place.

If we define "righteousness" in the customary manner, as moral virtue and ethical acheivement, then Jesus has no business—at least none of *God's* business—sitting at the same table with tax collectors and other moral criminals. But Matthew's Gospel wants us to see that righteousness is not an ethical achievement; it is first a gift of God's healing. We are all sinners. Do not romanticize it; do not psychologize it; and do not excuse it. In the light of the kingdom's radical demands ("You must be perfect, as your heavenly Father is perfect"—5:48), we are all pornographers and addicts to immorality, and if we are to be righteous, we don't need vain and hopeless appeals to our basic sense of decency. We need a physician of the soul. And that is precisely how this passage portrays Jesus (9:12).

So what is righteousness in the context of the kingdom? "Go study your Bible," Jesus told the Pharisees, "and there you will find it written, 'I desire mercy, and not sacrifice.' " The righteousness God desires is a life full of mercy, and God, who desires mercy, shows mercy through Jesus who "has authority on earth to forgive sins." So we gather, then, with other sinners at his table to discover a righteousness we cannot earn or grasp or merit through sacrifice, but a righteousness we can only receive as a gift of healing and then express through grateful lives of mercy and forgiveness to others. Indeed, it is only as forgiven disciples allow their lives to be claimed and shaped by the mercy of Christ that their "righteousness exceeds that of the scribes and the Pharisees" (5:20).

# The Fourth Sunday after Pentecost

| Lutheran | Roman Catholic | Episcopal | Common Lectionary |
|---|---|---|---|
| Exod. 19:2–8a | Exod. 19:2–6a | Exod. 19:2–8a | Gen. 25:19–34 |
| Rom. 5:6–11 | Rom. 5:6–11 | Rom. 5:6–11 | Rom. 5:6–11 |
| Matt. 9:35—10:8 | Matt. 9:36—10:8 | Matt. 9:35—10:8 | Matt. 9:35—10:8 |

## FIRST LESSON: EXODUS 19:2-8a

Exodus 19 contains the dramatic description of God's appearance (theophany) to Israel at Sinai, the startling overture to the announcement of the covenant between God and the people (chaps. 20–24). Scholars have rightly pointed out that the literary form of this section of Exodus parallels the typical pattern found in ancient Near-Eastern treaties between lords and their vassals. Moreover, echoes of primitive nature religion can be heard—the voice of God resounding in thunderstorms (19:16) and perhaps in volcanic eruptions (19:18).

The real power of this passage, however, lies neither in its historical connections to Near-Eastern diplomatic treaties nor in its pyrotechnic images, but in the sheer wonder of how it was that Israel came into being as a people. Every nation has some way of describing its origins. It points to a constitution or a revolution, to a monarch or a migration. And every nation tells of its birth with pride. "We were brave, resourceful, industrious, adventurous, and wise," say each nation's official historians. But Israel did not point to a constitution, but to a call and a covenant. Israel was born not by the design of resourceful leaders, but by the deliverance of a mighty God. The Hebrews were not strong; they were slaves. They were not politically clever; they were graciously chosen. They were not swept along by the tides of destiny; they were borne on eagles' wings and claimed by the Lord of all the earth (vv. 4-6).

Israel's formative national experience was like that of the weakest student suddenly summoned to the head of the class, the third-stringer astoundingly sent into the game at the critical moment, the bit character inserted into the leading role on opening night. The hand of God had fallen upon their shoulder: "You . . . you are the very one I choose."

But why? "You shall be to me a kingdom of priests and a holy nation" (v. 6). Israel was not to be the "teacher's pet;" they were to be a nation of ministers, a sign to all the peoples of the world that God is a deliverer of captives, a protector of the weak, a healer of the broken. The New Testament church understood itself to have been made a part of this covenant. "Consider your call," said Paul to the Corinthians. "Not many of you were wise . . . not many powerful . . . not many of noble birth; but God chose what is foolish in the world to shame the wise" (1 Cor. 1:26-27). The early Christians, too, knew themselves to be "a chosen race, a royal priesthood, a holy nation, God's own people." Why? So that they "may declare the wonderful deeds" of the God who called them from darkness to light (1 Peter 2:9). The church, too, as a servant community is called to be a "kingdom of priests and a holy nation."

A second-century Roman once described how the Christian church lived out its covenant identity in the world: "Although they live in Greek and barbarian cities . . . they never cease to witness to the reality of another city in which they live. . . . They are poor, and yet they make many rich; they are completely destitute, and yet they enjoy complete abundance. They are dishonored, and in their dishonor they are glorified; they are reviled, and yet they bless. . . . To put it simply: What the soul is in the body, that Christians are in the world."[5]

## ALTERNATIVE FIRST LESSON: GENESIS 25:19-34

"It wasn't worth the hassle!" That's a phrase contemporary people use to explain everything from failed relationships to why they avoided the shopping mall on a Saturday, or why they dropped chemistry in college.

Some things in life, after all, flatly do not justify the struggle, sweat, and stamina needed to secure them. Quite simply, they aren't worth the hassle.

What *is* worth the hassle? Or more deeply, what in life is worth an anguished struggle? That question rings throughout this text, which introduces a cycle of stories about one who was himself a world class struggler: *Jacob* (Genesis 25–35). The question is raised at the outset when we learn that Isaac's wife, Rebekah, is barren (vs. 21). Isaac is, of course, the child of the promise of God, the link between the word spoken to Abraham that he would become "a great nation" and the fulfillment of that word. From the beginning that fragile promise traveled a dangerous path, and now it has come to yet another dead end: Rebekah is barren. Is the promise worth the struggle? Isaac must decide, and his prayer on behalf of Rebekah (v. 21) signifies that the answer is yes. This prayer is no bland act of piety tossed off nonchalantly ("Thank you God for everything, and, oh yes, give Rebekah a baby. She wants one so badly.") This prayer is Isaac's struggle, his raiding of heaven through speech, his grasping for the blessing of God over against the cold, hard biological facts.

But then Rebekah herself must struggle. Her pregnancy was, as they say, a "hard" pregnancy (v. 22). She cries out in her pain, "If this is the way it is, then why should I live?" (v. 22), wondering if it is even worth living through such a painful pregnancy. She is now the one who raises the question: Is the promise worth the anguished struggle? So Rebekah takes her struggle to God, and she is told that her pain comes from the fact that she is carrying not one child, but two, and that she will become the mother not only of twins, but of rival nations. In other words, the struggle in her womb is worth it indeed since it is a sign and result of God's way of working in human history through suffering and struggle.

The struggle continues when the two children are born, the younger one, Jacob, grasping the heel of his older brother Esau (v. 26). They even adopt competing life-styles (v. 27—a hint of the enmity in the ancient world between shepherds and hunters) and divide their parents' loyalties (v. 28). And then comes the definitive scene. Esau the hunter, Esau the older son, Esau the inheritor of the birthright, comes in famished from the field and sells his birthright to Jacob for a bowl of "red stuff". "I am about to die," he wails hungrily. "Of what use is a birthright to me?" (v. 32).

The irony of that line would not be lost on early readers of Genesis. Genesis is the story of people going through spit, fire, and nails to hold on to the promise of God against all odds. Abraham left his homeland and his family, trusted God even in the face of Sarah's barrenness, and had his faith tested on Mount Moriah. Rebekah, too, left her homeland to become the wife of Isaac. Her own barrenness caused Isaac to plead with God that the promise of children and blessing would not come to an end, and her pregnancy had been rough, complicated, and perhaps even life-threatening. Two generations of people had torn themselves from their roots and headed out on a seemingly hopeless path of sacrifice, and all because of a promise: "I will make of you a great nation" (12:1). But now here is Esau, the older son, the rightful heir of the promise, standing there, licking his chops over a bowl of lentil stew and muttering, "Of what use is a birthright to me?" Basically, Esau is saying that the whole arduous history of faith that has led to this moment, to his own birth and to his possession of the promise, is simply not worth the hassle. The narrator provides a one-line spiritual obituary: "Thus Esau despised his birthright" (v. 34).

As for Jacob, he is a grasper and a wrestler, and we will learn in his story that his ethics are not always admirable. But his actions must be taken in the economy of this great narrative of the blessing of God. Seen from that vantage point, we can tell even at this early moment that Jacob, who hungers for the birthright more than food and drink, discerns what in life is truly worth the struggle.

## EPISTLE: ROMANS 5:6-11

Romans 5 begins with one of those famous Pauline "therefores." Paul has been developing an intricate argument about faith, and now he moves to a confessional summary: "Therefore, since we are justified by faith . . ." (5:1). What follows is a magnificent picture of the life of faithful people justified by God. It is a life which has been given "peace with God" and "access to grace." It is a life of "rejoicing," not only in the hope for the future, but also even in the sufferings of the present, which serve to increase hope (5:2-3). Moreover, "God's love has been poured into us through the Holy Spirit . . ." (5:5).

But then, the flow of words ceases; Paul's voice hesitates. One can almost see Tertius, the scribe (16:22), cocking his ear in Paul's direction, wondering why the crescendo of affirmations has suddenly grown silent. Perhaps Paul realized that his language could outrun his readers, that the more confident his words became the more perplexed his readers might grow. Perhaps Paul became aware that it was one thing to sing hymns of "rejoicing in hope" and "suffering leads to hope;" it was another thing to *believe* them.

In any case, Paul pauses to address the silent question, the implied doubt, of his readers: How can we be sure that God loves us? How do we know that our hope is not a vain, self-deceptive dream, and that it will not, as you say, Paul, "disappoint us"? (5:5). Everything rests, Paul responds, on the character of God. How do you know whether another person genuinely loves you? There is only one true test of character: You look at the way that person acts toward you. Just so, the only reliable way to know whether God truly loves us is to look at how God has acted toward us. And the news is good: "While we were yet sinners Christ died for us" (v. 8).

"Look at the face of a criminal," Karl Barth once said, "and you will see what God sees when he looks at us." God's love in Christ was not poured out because humanity finally elevated itself to some high moral plain, because humanity had anything to give in return, or because humanity was intrinsically lovable. To the contrary, it was precisely at the moment that humanity was in open and defiant rebellion, when criminal activity against the divine law was at its peak, that the love of God was most clearly and deeply revealed.

This display of love is without human parallel (v. 7), and it presses our minds to the limit to imagine it. Paul asks us to remember who we were— ungodly, sinners, enemies—and to gaze upon the cross. "Love so amazing, so divine," wrote Isaac Watts in "When I Survey the Wondrous Cross," "demands my soul, my life, my all." The God of love we see on the cross, the God who made peace with us when we were the ones—not God— waging war, this God who reconciled us is even now the God who lovingly stands with us and saves us in the midst of life (v. 10), giving us grace, joy, and hope. This is a God to be trusted. As one theologian stated, "The death of Christ could have been seen as the fate of a good life in a world dominated by evil persons. It could have been seen as an example of the way in which we are to respond to evil. The early Christian community, however, saw it neither as a terrible fate nor as a godly example, but as the redemptive act of God. . . . The atonement is the answer to George Bernard Shaw's contention that 'forgiveness is a beggar's refuge; we must pay our debts.' The debt . . . has been paid."[6]

### GOSPEL: MATTHEW 9:35—10:8

One of the regular features of *The New Yorker* magazine is an item called "Block That Metaphor," a brief column in which the editors catch politicians, broadcasters, reporters, and the like in the act of wildly mixing metaphors and creating outlandish and often amusing combinations of images. "Block That Metaphor" tells us of county officials who are described in the newspaper as "burying their heads in the sand, jumping to conclusions, and milking it for everything they can get," and reports on football coaches who say things like, "We're just gonna have to bite the bullet, take our medicine, and cross that bridge when we get to it. For now, though, we're gonna dance with the one who got us here."

At first reading, this passage from Matthew, in which Jesus sends out the twelve disciples to do ministry, appears to be a candidate for "Block That Metaphor." Observe how seemingly incompatible images are mixed.

Jesus' sending of the Twelve appears to be motivated by his compassion for the "harassed and helpless" crowds, who were "like sheep without a shepherd" (v. 36). Just as soon as Matthew has introduced this shepherding image, however, the metaphor gets mixed with another: field hands. "The harvest is plentiful," Jesus says as he prepares to commission the Twelve, "but the laborers are few; pray therefore the Lord of the harvest to send out laborers into his harvest" (9:37-38).

What, then, is the dominant picture of the Twelve as they move from the role of disciples (the learners) to that of apostles (the ones sent)? Are they sent out as shepherds to guide confused and wayward sheep, or as farm workers, armed with sickles, gathering in the ripe harvest? If we read on beyond the boundary of the lectionary text to 10:16, the images become even more complex: "Behold, I send you out as sheep in the midst of wolves; so be wise as serpents and innocent as doves." How shall we picture the identity of those whom Jesus sends? As shepherds? Harvesters? Sheep? Serpents? Doves? Block that metaphor!

There is no careless confusion, however, in this mixture of metaphors. Rather, there is a rich understanding of the nature of the ministry Jesus entrusts to the church. What is the ministry of disciples? It is the ministry of *shepherding*; the Twelve, and all disciples after them, are to go out as shepherds to the "lost sheep." They are to do the very same ministry Jesus did. With no regard for personal profit, they are to preach, to heal, and to guard the sheep from all the demonic and death-dealing powers that threaten them (vv. 7-8). This shepherding ministry brings not only tenderness and compassion, however; it also brings judgment. To preach "the kingdom of heaven is at hand" brings judgment upon all rival kingdoms. To be an ambassador for peace shakes the foundations of a society built upon enmity. To heal the sick and cleanse lepers, calls into question the comfortable arrangement of a world divided into the well and the sick, the haves and the have-nots. We know this is true from our own experience. The ministry of the kingdom stirs up opposition as well as gladness. Those who feed the hungry, clothe the naked, and house the homeless are more likely to become targets than society's heroes. Or when the ministry of Alcoholics Anonymous enables an alcoholic to move toward sobriety, sometimes this becomes a deep and troubling threat to those who have built their lives around the alcoholic's sickness. Shepherds of the kingdom seek restoration, but they may also divide the house (10:11-15).

That is why another image is needed, why the apostles are called "laborers of the harvest" as well as "shepherds." The preacher must not confuse the "harvest" image in this text with the cheerful picture of fruits and vegetables spilling out of a cornucopia on the cover of a Thanksgiving bulletin. In Matthew, the harvest is not a gentle image, but rather a symbol of the judgment, of the day when the sickle of God will divide the wheat from the weeds, and the weeds will be cast away and destroyed (see Matt. 13:36-43 and Joel 3:13). When Jesus sends the church into the world to do the ministry of the kingdom, he is not sending happy folks into an apple orchard to "pick your own." He is sending them into the tangled and confused field of the real world, where preaching the kingdom, ministering to the sick, speaking the message of peace, and showing mercy to the outcast are liable to be seen as world-subverting activities that will cause disciples to be delivered up to councils, lambasted in conventionally religious circles, and dragged before the powers that be (Matt. 10:17-18). They go out as shepherds; they will be treated like sheep in the midst of wolves. They go out as harvesters; they themselves are cut down with the sickle of persecution. What keeps them faithful is the promise that "the harvest will be plentiful" and the faith that the One who sends them is himself "the Lord of the harvest" (vv. 37-38).

# The Fifth Sunday after Pentecost

| Lutheran | Roman Catholic | Episcopal | Common Lectionary |
|----------|----------------|-----------|-------------------|
| Jer. 20:7–13 | Jer. 20:10–13 | Jer. 20:7–13 | Gen. 28:10–17 |
| Rom. 5:12–15 | Rom. 5:12–15 | Rom. 5:15b–19 | Rom. 5:12–19 |
| Matt. 10:24–33 | Matt. 10:26–33 | Matt. 10:24–33 | Matt. 10:24–33 |

### FIRST LESSON: JEREMIAH 20:7-13

Sometimes plays that are rousers off Broadway run into trouble when they hit the big stage. Take Jeremiah's two-act "Doom and Gloom" sermon, for example. Act One: Jeremiah holds a pottery vase high in the air and denounces Judah for idolatry and faithlessness. Act Two: Jeremiah smashes the vase into bits, shards, and fragments exploding toward the startled hearers, as the prophet warns, "Thus says the Lord of hosts: So will I break this people and this city." People out in the Valley of Hinnom had never seen a pulpit performance like that, and while reviews were surely mixed, Jeremiah at least provided the valley folk with a moment of high drama (Jeremiah 19). But when the prophet took his sermon into the city and tried an encore in the very temple court in Jerusalem, the critics were not so gentle. The curtain was barely up before the chief of the temple police jerked the hook and slapped Jeremiah in stocks (20:1-2). When the police chief released him the next day (20:3-6), Jeremiah gave the chief two gifts: a new name ("Instead of 'Chief of Police' you shall be called 'Sergeant Terror.' ") and a brief version of Act Two of "Doom and Gloom," minus the pottery ("You shall go into captivity in Babylon, and there you shall die").

The problem with Jeremiah's one-man show was that it was both negative and ill-timed. People prefer "Sweetness and Light" to "Doom and Gloom," especially when there seems to be no cause for alarm. Most people were optimistic about Judah's national fortunes. Economic forecasts were generally cheery, and the reports of military stirrings to the east in Babylon seemed remote. Basically, then, there was no reason for anybody to take Jeremiah's dire warnings seriously, and it was the out-of-sync character of Jeremiah's message that gave rise to today's lesson.

The text is one of several psalmlike, poetic laments that punctuate the book of Jeremiah. Although this text may have at one time been an independent literary unit, it has been placed here in the framework of the book of Jeremiah to make a theological point. Jeremiah complains that the Lord had tricked him into crying "violence and destruction" when all around there is nothing but sunny good cheer (vv. 7-9). Jeremiah cries that he would like to keep his mouth shut, but the Lord's message burns like a fire in his bones (v. 9). As is the case with many personal laments, however, the attitude of the lamenter changes as the poem proceeds. Jeremiah moves from charging God with deceit to an appeal to God for vindication. He recognizes that everybody around him is relishing his downfall, and he closes the lament with an anguished, but nevertheless confident, prayer to the Lord as his only hope for deliverance (vv. 10-13).

Theologically, this passage goes beyond the experience of Jeremiah to raise the issue of the relationship of God's Word to the evidence at hand. The gospel always possesses a certain "out-of-place, out-of-time" quality. Sometimes, like Jeremiah, the church is called to speak a word of warning and judgment to a culture (and to itself) floating merrily along at ease. When the world is in a party mood, when houses are filled with microwave ovens and happy images flash across television screens, any call for repentance, any notion that values are shaky and destruction lies close at hand, seems ill-timed to say the least and an occasion for ridicule.

It is not, however, only the judgment side of the gospel that seems out of place. The gospel announces grace and comfort into those places in life where nothing at hand supports such a word. "Blessed" is the word the gospel gives to the poor in spirit, to the meek, to the peacemakers, and

to those who mourn. "I am the resurrection and the life," is the word of
the Lord at graveside in the face of death. Such messages, like Jeremiah's,
seem hollow and false, but because they are true they cannot be held in.
The church can only risk scorn by speaking them and pray with all its
might to the Lord who "delivers the life of the needy" (v. 13).

### ALTERNATIVE FIRST LESSON: GENESIS 28:10-17

"We are climbing Jacob's ladder . . . ," goes the old spiritual, and this
account of Jacob's dream, with angel's ascending and descending a ladder
to heaven, may well be the best known of all the Jacob stories. At least
three aspects of this text demand our attention. First, historically the story
may have developed as a way of explaining the origins of the ancient
sanctuary at Bethel. After the division of the northern and southern kingdoms, Bethel became an important worship site in the north. Judah had
the temple, but Israel had Bethel (which means "House of God"). This
Jacob story reinforced the idea that Bethel was not inferior to the temple,
but rather had been a sacred place from the earliest times. Beyond this
historical conjecturing, though, there is the theological idea that sanctuaries
are places of sacred worship in part because they are places of sacred
*memory*.

Some denominations, for example, encourage the holding of funerals
in the regular place of worship rather than in funeral homes, not because
God is confined to any sanctuary, but instead because the sanctuary is the
place where other sacred events have taken place. Here in the place of
baptisms, marriages, and ordinations; here where the gospel is preached
and heard and the Lord's table spread; here where generations have on
countless occasions exclaimed, like Jacob, "The Lord is in this place!"
here is where the ending of life should be commemorated and the witness
to the resurrection proclaimed anew.

Second, in this story of Jacob's dream, the promise of God is reaffirmed,
this time in the life of the trickster Jacob (vv. 13-15). The first portion of
the promise formula (vv. 13-14) is familiar, even predictable. God promises
to Jacob land and descendants, the same things pledged to Abraham (12:1-
2) and Isaac (26:3), but now a new element is added. Verse 15 begins with
the word "behold," a signal to Jacob (and to the reader) to perk up and
pay attention since something unexpected is about to emerge (see, for
example, the "behold" in Gen. 22:13). "Behold, I am with you and will
keep you wherever you go. . . . I will not leave you." The reader of
Genesis has already learned enough about Jacob to realize his crafty ways,
his tendency toward sleight-of-hand methods, and this gives God's new
promise a double meaning. God is vowing not to let this schemer "out of

sight," but God is also promising not to forsake even the wily Jacob, to gather the life of even this sly fox into the great and redemptive promise.

Third, the account of Jacob's dream must be held in tension with the story of Jacob's other nighttime encounter with God, the wrestling match at Jabbok (Gen. 32:22-32). Jacob's dream is a magnificent vision. God, the promise, angels, a ladder between heaven and earth, all of these combine into an account of compelling beauty and power. And yet it must be said that Jacob leaves this moment as the same old Jacob. Even his post-dream speech bears all the marks of the old wheeler-dealer: "If God will give me everything I need, then the Lord shall be my God." You scratch my back; I'll scratch yours.

When Jacob meets God on that other night, however, he leaves wounded and changed, blessed and given a new name: Israel. He walks away from his wrestling with God with a limp and a new identity. The dream of Bethel found reality at Jabbok. In his dream, Jacob heard the ancient promise of God and discovered that this promise was for him, too. Beside the river Jabbok that painful, struggle-filled night, Jacob discovered how it is that the promises of God are fulfilled through suffering. Jacob's story anticipates the story of Jesus. Jesus, too, was the bearer of the promise, and the promise that led Jacob from Bethel to Jabbok was the same promise that led Jesus from Bethlehem to Gethsemane and Golgotha.

The church also has received the promise that Jacob received at Bethel: "I am with you always, to the close of the age" (Matt. 28:20). And the way of this promise is, as it always has been, the way of suffering. "The one who does not take up a cross and follow me is not worthy of me" (Matt. 10:38). Anyone who sings, "We are climbing Jacob's ladder . . ." must remember the next line: ". . . soldiers of the cross."

## EPISTLE: ROMANS 5:12-19

At first glance this passage appears to be as vague and abstract a piece of theological writing as one could possibly expect to find. It looks like the description of the moves in some metaphysical chess match. First we encounter Adam, or at least the Adam who stands as a representative of all humanity. Adam, as is well known, disobeyed God, and through this one man's trespass "sin came into the world . . . and death through sin" (v. 12). But, then, Jesus Christ, who is also a representative of all humanity, comes into play. Adam sinned, but through Christ's obedience all people receive "acquittal and life" (v. 17). So, we have a series of opposing moves: Adam—disobedience, Christ—obedience; Adam—sin, Christ—righteousness; Adam—condemnation, Christ—justification; Adam—death, Christ—life. Checkmate.

The fact is, though, Paul is not merely playing chess with religious concepts nor working on a problem in theological calculus. He is speaking about the realities of human life, everybody's life. Adam's disobedience is not some distant event that somehow gets arbitrarily placed upon the shoulders of each new generation. *Everybody* sins (v. 12); to do so is both the destiny and the choice of every human being. The minister and theologian Carlyle Marney was once asked where the Garden of Eden was located. "215 Elm Street, Knoxville, Tennessee,"[7] he replied, giving the address of his childhood home. It was there, explained Marney, that he first stole, and hid, and lied, and was found out. "Adam" is everywoman . . . everyman, and all of the alienation, betrayal, selfishness, and falsehood that infect human life are signs of a deeper separation from God. Human beings, claims Paul, essentially and thoroughly, reject God. The law did not call a halt to this rejection; to the contrary, it kept score of the abuses (v. 20).

How does God respond to this rejection? In Jesus Christ God rejects the rejection. In Christ God reaches out to reclaim humanity as God's own. The deepest intention of human disobedience, claimed Karl Barth, "is to deny that God is really God and really love. . . . Humanity may be hostile to the gospel of God, but this gospel is not hostile to humanity." In the face of that hostile disobedience, God responds by loving, by taking sin and death into the very heart of God and overcoming them, and by setting human beings free to live once again (v. 17). Nothing—not death, not powers, not principalities—nothing will be allowed to stand in the way of the love of God, reclaiming humanity in Jesus Christ. The result is not a balancing act—Adam on one side of the scale, Christ on the other, everything evened out. To the contrary, the result is not balance, but an *abundance* of grace. If the "old Adam" brought destruction, how *much more* through the "new Adam" will grace and righteousness overflow (v. 17).

The joke, then, is on sin and death. Centuries of sinister work for nothing! Countless generations of people infected, only to be healed by the grace of God! Foolproof snares of destruction, sprung open through Christ's liberating obedience! And now, beginning to rise in an ever-insistent chorus, not the music of despair and woe, but the laughter of the redeemed, and the mocking hymns of the faithful, "O death, where is thy victory? O death, where is thy sting? Thanks be to God who gives us the victory through our Lord Jesus Christ" (1 Cor. 15:55-57).

### GOSPEL: MATTHEW 10:24-33

In this passage Jesus continues his instructions to the Twelve, begun in v. 1, as he sends them out to do ministry. Jesus is the speaker; the disciples are the audience; but Matthew aims this text at his own readers. They knew well what Jesus meant when he told his disciples that they "would be hated by all for my sake" (v. 22). Matthew's church had experienced persecution, and Jesus' warnings of rejection and violence had been fulfilled in their own experience. Matthew wants his readers to know that the pain they are suffering is to be expected. Jesus suffered rejection, and his followers must not be surprised by conflict with the world, for "the servant (is) like his master" (v. 25). Indeed, "if they have called the master of the house Beelzebul (a reference to 9:34 and an anticipation of 12:24), how much more will they malign those of his household" (v. 25). In other words, if the opponents of the kingdom called Jesus demon-possesed, they will surely hurl the same charge, and more, at his followers.

In some parts of the world, preachers will have no difficulty seeing the relevance of this text. In many societies, Christians still pay a costly price for their witness, and this passage speaks directly to their painful experience. Other Christians, however, seem far removed from the world of violence and persecution. Jesus may have been hated and rejected in his day, but Christians today are often benignly tolerated, at worst, and, at best, celebrated as good citizens. They are in all the civic clubs, their ministers are invited to pray at football games, and they are even elected to high political office.

There is reason to rejoice, of course, over any society that practices religious freedom and toleration. Christians do not seek persecution, as if being ridiculed and rejected by the society were some meritorious badge of righteousness. On the other hand, faithfulness to the call of Jesus Christ will always create tension with the values and practices of the larger culture. In some societies, Christians are called into court and thrown into prison; in all societies, the claims of Christians are called into question and thrown into doubt.

Take, for example, the Christian conviction that love is stronger than hatred, and mercy more powerful than retribution. There is plenty of evidence at hand that such convictions are nothing more than impractical and romantic gibberish. Power in our world is not *really* gained through love and mercy, but through muscle, manipulation, fear, domination, and cold cash. Anyone who relies upon love and mercy as a base of power is simply living in another world. One of the aides of South African Bishop Tutu candidly expressed his impatience with the bishop's tolerance. "At his age you'd think he would have learned to hate a little more," he said. "But there is this problem with Tutu: he believes literally in the gospel."[8]

It is at this point that the text becomes pertinent to Christians in all times and places. To be a disciple of Jesus Christ means obeying another authority than the spirit of the present age. Living in the light of God's kingdom is,

in the deepest sense possible, "living in another world," the hidden world
of God's reign. To the present age the kingdom life-style seems to be a
foolish waste. Its truth is hidden from view; its power is covered from
sight. Jesus is promising his disciples that, when the final verdict about
human life is given, "nothing is covered that will not be revealed, or hidden
that will not be known" (v. 26).

The world, claims Jesus, sees only "the body." To the world, might
makes right, and the main occupation of human beings is to "look out for
number one." From that perspective, "blessed are the merciful" (5:7) is
a romantic trifle and "love your enemies" (5:44) an invitation to foolish-
ness. Jesus is proclaiming, however, that the future belongs not to the
world, which has power only over the body, but to God, who holds the
body and the soul (v. 28). What the world considers worthless ( "Are not
two sparrows sold for a penny?"—v. 29) and of little count (who numbers
the "hairs of your head"?—v. 30) are of great value to God.

# The Sixth Sunday after Pentecost

| Lutheran | Roman Catholic | Episcopal | Common Lectionary |
|---|---|---|---|
| Jer. 28:5–9 | 2 Kings 4:8–11, 14–16a | Isa. 2:10–17 | Gen. 32:22–32 |
| Rom. 6:1b–11 | Rom. 6:3–4, 8–11 | Rom. 6:3–11 | Rom. 6:3–11 |
| Matt. 10:34–42 | Matt. 10:37–42 | Matt. 10:34–42 | Matt. 10:34–42 |

### FIRST LESSON: JEREMIAH 28:5-9

It's easy to tell the charlatans, the Elmer Gantrys, and the con artists on
the religious scene, but how do we distinguish between true and false
prophecy? The hucksters and flimflam preachers are obvious parodies of
the truth. They cry on camera cue, hawk religious trinkets, promise miracles
for money, build temples to their own egos, and turn the church into a
massage parlor of greed. They can be spotted a mile away. But how do
we tell the difference between two apparently genuine prophets, between
the truth of God's Word and a word that appears to be God's word, a word

that seems to ring true, but does not in fact come from the Lord? This is a major and perennial problem in the life of the community of faith, and it is the concern of this text.

The situation is as follows: It is August of 594 B.C., and the dreaded superpower Babylon is in control of Judah. Three years earlier, the Babylonian king Nebuchadnezzar, in an effort to solidify his political power, had moved his armies into Palestine, and in March of 597 B.C., Jerusalem fell. So, the capital of Judah has been captured, the Temple has been stripped of its sacred furnishings, a puppet king named Zedekiah is on the throne, and Nebuchadnezzar is calling the political shots.

So what did God have to say about all of this? Was there a "Word from the Lord"? The prophets were of two minds about this. On the one hand, some of the prophets were persuaded that God was displeased that pagan Babylon had risen to power and that the fortunes of Judah would soon be restored. "Take heart, Judah. Your trials will soon be over." This was one version of the word from the Lord. This was a theologically optimistic and potent view because, after all, these prophets had the Scripture on their side. God had promised David never to forsake the royal house (2 Sam. 7:14); discipline, yes, but abandon, no, never. Hananiah was one of these prophets, and his sermon in the bare Temple had all the marks of true prophecy (Jer. 28:14). "Thus says the Lord of hosts, the God of Israel," he began. "I have broken the yoke of the king of Babylon. Within two years I will bring back the furnishings of the temple and restore the royal house." So, according to Hananiah, God had some bad news and some good news for Judah. The bad news was that the evil Babylonians would be around for two more years, but the good news was that it was only to be two years, then things would be back to normal around Jerusalem.

On the other hand, there was Jeremiah, and according to him the word from the Lord was "bad news, worse news." Jeremiah was convinced that, far from stopping the Babylonian humiliation of Judah, God had *caused* it (Jer. 27:6). Not only that, Judah was in for a long occupation and the future was even more grave than the present (28:12-16).

Now, who's telling the truth—Hananiah or Jeremiah? Both were evidently earnest, both could quote Scripture on their behalf, both had credentials as prophets, both began their sermons, "Thus says the Lord. . . ." How do we distinguish between the authentic word from God and the false word? There are, of course, no foolproof tests, but our text gives us three clues:

First, notice that Jeremiah, when he hears Hananiah's comforting prophecy, basically responds, "Amen, I hope you're right" (v.6). Some so-called prophets relish the chance to speak the hard word to people and enjoy the "prophetic" stance of lashing out at others for their sins. It costs them nothing, since they feel superior to the people, and their prophecies carry the odor of condescension. Jeremiah, however, derived no personal pleasure from Judah's pain. Indeed, as a member of the community, he shared their pain. A true prophet comes from the community of faith and deeply cares for its well-being. A true prophet has the courage to speak judgment when it is God's truth, but also prays like mad that judgment will be tempered with mercy.

Second, Jeremiah appealed to the past, to the prophetic tradition, to the broad history of God's speaking to the people (vv. 7-9). God's prophetic word in the present is consistent with the actions and character of God in the past. Hananiah could appeal to Israel's past, but his message of painless restoration showed that his historical memory was highly selective. He was like the synagogue congregation Jesus addressed at Nazareth who liked their prophecy edited for comfort. They enjoyed hearing Jesus preach on the "good news" passage from Isaiah, but they became enraged at the memory of those times when the prophetic word came as judgment (Luke 4:16-30). Across the generations, true prophecy has maintained the tension between divine judgment and grace, the word of comfort and the word of suffering, a call to repentance and the promise of restoration.

Finally, Jeremiah reminds Hananiah that prophets who cry "peace" must be placed under special scrutiny (v. 9). This is not because God does not promise peace (indeed Jeremiah himself will later prophesy the restoration of Judah—chap. 31), but rather it is because God's peace is always given in the midst of suffering. False prophets and their hearers are prone to cosmetic cures rather than healing, to say "Peace, peace" when there is no peace. So it is with all today who encourage "positive thinking" and provide easy, cross-free assurances that "God will take care of us." When Jesus entered Jerusalem and heard the crowds singing of peace, he wept. With his eye already on Calvary, he said, "I wish you knew the things that make for peace" (Luke 19:42).

### ALTERNATIVE FIRST LESSON: GENESIS 32:22-32

One commentator has observed that this text is like an old house which had many owners. Each owner added a room to the house, and in a different style of architecture. As for the final result: Some people love it, some people hate it, but all are impressed by its uniqueness. In terms of meaning, this text is, in many ways, as murky as that shadowy night by the river it describes.

The story comes as Jacob is on his way to a crucial meeting with his estranged brother Esau. Jacob is fearful of Esau's potentially murderous rage, and in his fear he prays a typically Jacob-like prayer: "Deliver me, I pray thee, from the hand of my brother . . . for I fear him. . . . But thou didst say, 'I will do you good, and make your descendents as the sand of the sea. . . .' " (32:12). Here is Jacob, the old stew broker and shell game artist, pulling out the contract in a moment of crisis to remind God that he did, after all, sign on the dotted line and promise to make Jacob the father of many descendents.

Jacob expects to encounter Esau, and he does, but not before he encounters another, unexpected, opponent. Perhaps the best way to understand what this strange meeting is about is not to attempt to explain every detail, but rather to focus upon what resulted from it:

First, Jacob received a new name: Israel. Although the etymology of the name "Israel" is not absolutely clear, it possesses a definite theological character ("God Rules" or "God Protects" are fair guesses). Moreover, a name in ancient times was intimately linked with personal identity. So, we don't just have Jacob with a new name; we have a new Jacob. He is, like Saul who became Paul and Simon who became Peter, God's man in a new and more intimate way. Some commentators have noted that the very ambiguity of this story (Was it God alone with whom Jacob wrestled, or was Esau or even Jacob's inner self the opponent, too? Perhaps all three.) Is the narrator's way of protecting the mystery of God's involvement in human life. We all wrestle with God, ourselves, our past, and all at once. Whenever we emerge into the light from the dimness of that struggle to discover that we have been given a new "name," a new identity, a new way of being in the world, we give thanks to God, while at the same time not trying to sort out which part of our wrestling was human and which divine.

Second, Jacob received a wound, a limp. Most nations do not remember the flaws of their heroes, and if they do they don't celebrate them in legend. George Washington surely fibbed as much as the next person, but in the popular legend he "could not tell a lie." But whenever the people of Israel told their legends, they remembered that the great and savvy and strong Jacob spent the last years of his life dragging one leg lamely along after the other. Through this primitive story of its origins, Israel remembered what the church, in its time, has also learned, that to draw near to God is also to share in suffering. We "share Christ's sufferings" said the writer of 1 Peter (4:13), and we are "fellow heirs with Christ," wrote Paul, "provided we suffer with him" (Rom. 8:17). It was also Paul who prayed that his own "limp," his "thorn in the flesh" be removed, and the answer he received was, "My grace is sufficient for you, for my power is made perfect in weakness" (2 Cor. 12:9). One of the earliest biblical signs of that truth is the picture of Jacob, now Israel, limping on the far side of the river toward his meeting with Esau.

Third, Jacob received restoration with Esau. Although the account of their reconciliation is beyond the boundaries of this text (see 33:1-17), our text clearly points toward it. We cannot grant too much of the credit for this healing to Jacob; though he gives Esau gifts, he seems to get much more than he gave. But such is always the case with those who "have seen God face to face" (v. 30).

(For additional information on this text, see the comments on Genesis 28:10-17 [Alternative First Lesson, The Fifth Sunday after Pentecost], pp. 36-37.)

## EPISTLE: ROMANS 6:1b-11

Every time somebody belts out the hymn "Amazing Grace," somebody else whispers, "Does that mean we can do whatever we want?" Every time someone argues, as Paul does in the early chapters of Romans, that God is a benevolent, merciful, gift-giving God who freely lavishes grace on humanity, the specter of irresponsible human liberty is conjured up: Human beings wheeling recklessly down the highway of forgiveness, the top down, doing whatever they please, running amok on God's charge card, confident that if they should wreck their lives, God's kindly hand will put them behind the wheel of something shiny and new. "I love to sin," begins the famous statement of Heinrich Heine. "God loves to forgive sin. Really, this world is admirably arranged."[9]

Far from avoiding this problem of the relationship between grace and human responsibility, Paul brings it up himself and faces it directly. In Romans 5, Paul has argued that the depths of human sin served not to defeat the purposes of God, but rather opened up the artesian well of overflowing grace. The deeper sin drilled into the crust of human life, the more God's mercy flowed from the wound (5:20). Having said that, Paul then turns in the sixth chapter to the obvious rejoinder: "What shall we say then? Are we to continue in sin that grace may abound?" (v. 1). In other words, if sin is the means by which we tap the resources of grace, should we drive the bit of sin down deeper to allow grace to well up more fully?

Notice, however, that when Paul provides an answer to his own question, he effectively *changes* the question. The question he posed was, "What should we *do*?" This is a question about ethical strategy. The answer he gives, though, is to a different question: "Who *are* we?" This is a question of Christian identity. Paul points to Christian baptism, possibly employing words and images from the baptismal liturgy to describe a change that has taken place in the lives of people of faith. To be baptized, Paul maintains, is to be "united with Christ" (v. 5) in two ways: in his death and in his resurrection. This does not imply some fuzzy kind of mystical union by which Christians run around as "little Jesuses." Being united with Christ, rather, points to the mighty act of God in Jesus Christ in which the old age of sin and death was destroyed and the new age of life and righteousness was inaugurated. God in Christ cut the chains that bound humanity to the old death-filled world, and God in Christ created a new world of peace between God and humanity. To be united with Christ in death and in resurrection is to be delivered from the old world to the new, from Egypt to the Promised Land, from slavery to freedom.

So, if you want an answer to the question "Should we continue to sin . . .?" asserts Paul, ask instead, "Who are we, and where do we live?" Are we still slaves? No. Do we still live in bondage? No. We have been carried through the waters of baptism into the new land of promise, into the new life of Christ (vv. 5-11). Considering the possibility of continuing in sin is, in effect, casting our eyes back to Egypt.

The fact is, though, that human beings do continue to sin, and human life is still marred by brokenness and death. The fullness of our redemption lies ahead of us, in God's future. This does not mean, though, that freedom from sin is merely a pie-in-the-sky ideal with no present ethical consequences. The Christian life is a stained and broken attempt to live out the identity we have already been given in and through Christ. There will be many failures, to be sure, in all human attempts to live as those who belong to God, but the grace of God means not only that we are delivered from death; it also means, wonder of wonders, that even now our lives can rise here and there, now and then, above our selfish desires and our hollow idolatries and become obedient signs of God's reign of peace (v. 11).

### GOSPEL: MATTHEW 10:34-42

A New Testament scholar once remarked about a particularly troublesome text, "This is one of those things I wish Jesus had never said." Well, here is another one. Most of us would probably be just as pleased if Jesus had never proclaimed, as he does in this passage, that the purpose of his coming was to set people against their parents, in-laws, spouses, and children. Many hours of pastoral care are devoted to patching up family quarrels, cooling the angry rhetoric, and achieving some sort of truce between warring family members. Here is Jesus, however, seemingly telling us that his mission is not to stop family fights, but to *start* them. What do we make of this?

Most preachers probably try to wriggle off the hook, either by avoiding the text altogether or by softening its force. Matthew, they remind us, was composed in a missionary situation, and Christians in Matthew's context were almost always converts from other religions. These conversions often created strife between the new Christian and the rest of the family, who neither understood nor approved of this dramatic change. So, Matthew included this statement by Jesus in order to reassure his church that such family conflict over their newfound faith was to be expected. Moreover, Jesus was not really speaking out *against* families; he just says that we should love him *more* than families (never mind that Luke's version of this text, probably closer to the original language, calls upon us to "hate" our families—Luke 14:26).

So goes the softening approach. There is truth in this argument, of course, but it finally ends up sanding the text smooth, diminishing its startling and radical claim. If we look honestly at this passage, we must acknowledge that Jesus is not just gently reminding us to keep our priorities straight—God first, family second, self third. The vocabulary of this passage is the language of battle: "I have come not to bring peace, but a sword. . . . I have come to set a person against loved ones . . . your own household will be your foes . . . those who find their lives will lose them. . . ." Jesus is demanding a costly, painful, conflict-generating obedience to himself and to the kingdom he proclaimed.

So what do we have here? Is Jesus advocating the breakup of families and brawls with parents and in-laws? No, in fact later in Matthew Jesus claims that it is God who joins men and women together in marriage (19:6) and cites with approval the commandment "honor your father and mother" (19:19). The crucial issue in this text has to do with the breaking in of the kingdom of heaven in the ministry and life of Jesus. Now two worlds lie side by side, the old world and the kingdom, and people must decide in which of these worlds they will live. That may seem like an easy choice— why, the kingdom, of course!—except for the fact that the old world still retains considerable power to give meaning to life. One can find in the old world friends, family, love, work, and even religion. The crisis of the old world is not that it is empty and meaningless, but that it is *obsolete*. The new world is God's future coming into being, and it does violence to the old world, which will pass away. The old world can provide structure and meaning, but only the kingdom brings life. The old world can provide temporary shelter, but only the life of the kingdom leads home.

Jesus, then, does not call on us to turn our backs on those we love. He calls us to turn our backs on the old world, on all attempts to make ultimate meaning out of commitments other than our commitment to the kingdom, even our most intimate and loving relationships. As ethicist Stanley Hauerwas states, "Now that we are in the presence of Jesus Christ, all our relations have been transvalued. In the death and resurrection of this man, a great reversal has taken place, causing all our natural loves to be transformed." [10]

Some people love their families, their jobs, their life-styles, themselves *instead of* Christ. For them, the kingdom comes like a sword, cutting away all attempts to rest faith in these lesser, old world, loyalties. Important as these aspects of life are, they are not the ultimate reality, and they cannot make us fully human. Other people love their familes, jobs, life-styles, and selves *alongside* Christ. For them, the kingdom also comes as a sword, slicing away the illusion that life can be compartmentalized that way. Christ is not one reality among many; Christ is the ultimate reality from which all life flows. Only when a person abandons (is "set against", becomes a "foe" of) all attempts to derive ultimate meaning in that which is not ultimate can true life and meaning be found. "He who finds his life will lose it, and he who loses his life for my sake will find it" (v. 39). Only when we allow the sword of Christ's kingdom to sever our ties to our little kingdoms, only when we lose our lives for Christ's sake, do we truly receive life. Only then do we know *how* to love, and only then can we love our families, our friends, and even our enemies *through* Christ and *because* of Christ, and not instead of or alongside of Christ.

# The Seventh Sunday after Pentecost

| Lutheran | Roman Catholic | Episcopal | Common Lectionary |
|----------|----------------|-----------|-------------------|
| Zech. 9:9–12 | Zech. 9:9–10 | Zech. 9:9–12 | Exod. 1:6–14, 22—2:10 |
| Rom. 7:15–25a | Rom. 8:9, 11–13 | Rom. 7:21—8:6 | Rom. 7:14–25a |
| Matt. 11:25–30 | Matt. 11:25–30 | Matt. 11:25–30 | Matt. 11:25–30 |

## FIRST LESSON: ZECHARIAH 9:9-12

Little is known about the origins of this text. The RSV translation applies the generic title "An Oracle" to all of chapters 9–10, but whose oracle it is, we do not know. It is included in the book of sayings and visions of the prophet Zechariah, who was active from 520–518 B.C., but this "oracle" seems to come from a later, but difficult-to-pinpoint, time. It bears some similarities in content to the authentic Zechariah material, but it derives from another hand in another place and time. Just when and where, we cannot say. Our text, then, seems to float above any identifiable historical circumstance, and indeed, the main preaching value of this text over the years has been the fact that it is a gold mine of themes and images that reappear in the New Testament.

The first of these images comes as something of a dramatic surprise. Chapter 9 opens up with drums, bugles, and divine saber-rattling. God the warrior is stirring in the heavenly places and sending out a warning to all those nations who are "squatting" on Israel's land, the promised land, to prepare to be cleared away in battle (9:1-8). One can almost hear the stamping of feet as the Lord's army of liberation approaches; one can almost see the dust clouds just over the horizon as God's mighty troops advance toward Israel. But then . . . God's army comes into view, and instead of streams of troops in battle array, there is but one lone figure. Instead of waves of horses and chariots, there is but one beast, a lowly colt. Behold this strange army of liberation: "Lo, your king comes to you; triumphant and victorious is he, humble and riding on an ass . . ." (v. 9). It is this image, the picture of the God whose power is meekness and whose liberation comes through apparent weakness, that was employed by the early church to interpret Jesus' identity as he entered into Jerusalem (Matt. 21:5).

The second image is that of the God who wages, not war, but peace for the nations (v. 10). Earthly kings use armed hostilities to conquer nations. God conquers hostility on behalf of the nations. In the New Testament this theme is applied to Jesus Christ in such passages as Ephesians 2:14-17 ("He is our peace . . .") and Colossians 1:20 (". . . making peace by the blood of his cross").

The final image is that of the "blood of the covenant" as God's promise to set captives free, to fulfill eager hopes, and to restore the people (v. 12). The phrase "blood of the covenant" hearkens back to the time when Moses read aloud the words of the covenant and then cast the sacrificial blood upon the people of Israel (Exodus 24:7-8). The early church linked this to Jesus' own sacrifice and believed that the "blood of the covenant" was cast upon them each time they celebrated the Lord's Supper: "Drink of it, all of you; for this is my blood of the covenant, which is poured out for many for the forgiveness of sins" (Matt. 26:27-28).

### ALTERNATIVE FIRST LESSON: EXODUS 1:6-14, 22—2:10

This text has been strangely edited in the lectionary. What we get is the account of Joseph's death (1:6), the growth of the Hebrew population in Egypt (1:7), the beginnings of Hebrew slavery (1:8-14), and the account of Moses' birth (1:22—2:10). What gets left out is the story of the clever actions of the two Hebrew midwives (1:15-21), and along with it one of the most important keys to understanding this section of Exodus.

In order to get at this understanding, we need to note that two central contrasts in this entire passage are those between the *strong and the weak* and between *men and women.* A new Pharaoh (male, of course) now rules in Egypt (1:8), and he announces his intention to "deal shrewdly" with the Hebrews living in the land, lest they become too powerful (1:10). His first shrewd plan was to use his strength to make slaves of the Hebrews, but this scheme backfires because the more the Hebrews "were oppressed, the more they multiplied" (1:12).

Pharaoh clearly needs another "shrewd" plan, and this time it is genocide. He orders the two Hebrew midwives, Shiphrah and Puah, to kill newborn Hebrew infants—not *all* of them, just the "important" ones, the males (1:15-16). But these two women, because they feared God (1:17), defied the power of Pharaoh and let the male children live. When Pharaoh interrogated them about this, they concocted a story about Hebrew women being so strong that they deliver their babies before the midwives can get to the scene, and thus outwitted "shrewd" Pharaoh (1:18-20).

So Pharaoh develops yet another "shrewd" strategy: genocide, plan B. This time the general populace is ordered to throw all male Hebrew babies into the Nile (1:22). This plan, too, is thwarted, again by women, and the result is the preservation of the life of Moses (2:1-10).

The message of the whole text is clear. All that seems strong and invincible is undermined by that which seems weak and of no account. Masculine, calculating, godless Pharaoh is played for the fool by weak, God-fearing women. All of his shrewd schemes are destroyed by even shrewder women; all of his defensive plots to oppress only yield greater strength for the people of God. "God chose what is foolish in the world to shame the wise, God chose what is weak in the world to shame the strong, God chose what is low and despised in the world, even things that are not, to bring to nothing things that are" (1 Cor. 1:27-28). The church, then, dares to believe that its foolish life—a life of welcoming strangers to potluck suppers, praying for the dying, gathering clothing and food for the poor, visiting the castoffs in prison, teaching the story of faith to its children, and preaching the gospel of hope—is more real and more enduring than the chariots, gold, and shrewdness of all Pharaohs past and present.

## EPISTLE: ROMANS 7:14-25a

"We know God will forgive our sins," states a character in one of Peter De Vries's novels. "The question is what God will think of our virtues."[11] This is precisely the question faced by Paul in this famous passage from Romans. Here Paul struggles with the deepest mystery of the ethical life: how the earnest desire to do good can lead instead to evil.

The experiential centerpiece of this text is the astonished statement, "I do not understand my own actions. For I do not do what I want, but I do the very thing I hate" (v. 15). What is Paul talking about here? Some have suggested that Paul is speaking of the familiar human struggle against temptation. The alcoholic wants to be sober but cannot resist the morning "eye-opener." The neighbor wishes to be kind, but the latest gossipy scandal is simply too delicious not to spread. The politician wants to be fair and just, but the temptation to play favorites on the new building contract is just too strong. It is true that this is a tendency in human behavior, but this is not what Paul has in mind.

What Paul is describing is not the failure to live up to our ideals, but something far more sinister in human life. Paul is describing the bewilderment and shock that occur when, in fact, people *do* live up to the ideal only to discover that the result is devastating evil. Ordinary experience is full of apt examples. Attempts to protect the environment end up damaging the seas and atmosphere even more. Weapons engineered to provide national security produce global danger. A drug designed to give fertility to childless couples yields the tragedy of deformed babies. A highway planned to bring economic prosperity destroys a thriving neighborhood. Programs to end poverty create helpless dependency and despair. Parents trying to give their offspring the best that life can offer produce aimless, alienated, and angry children. Everyone, at some point in life, can join in Paul's astonished cry, "I do not understand my own actions. I did not create what I wanted; I created the very thing I hate."

It must be said, though, that Paul is addressing a concern even more profound than these experiences from workaday life. Pressed to the deepest level, human beings at their best desire to be at one with God. That is the ultimate good in human life. For Paul, the highest expression of this good was a life lived according to the law of God—not the law as an oppressive set of "dos and don'ts," but the law as the joyous means of being in the world and with God. But even the law, which "is good" (v. 16), has been sucked under the malevolent control of sin, so that all human attempts to make peace with God by living the law produce, strangely and sadly, the very opposite result: gripping guilt and deeper alienation from God (vv. 22-23). "I am never as dangerous," Reinhold Niebuhr said, "as when I act in love." [12] Here is the most tragic dimension in life: When human beings are trying their hardest to be religious, when human beings are trying their best to do God's will through their own moral force, it is then, ironically, that they become most lost, most under the power of sin, most "Godless." We see this in the Gospels in Jesus' conflicts with the Pharisees, who are not evil people, but people striving with all their might to do the good, and generating children of hell instead (Matt. 23:15). "What a person wants is salvation," writes Ernst Käsemann. "What he creates is a disaster." [13]

"Wretched man that I am! Who will deliver me from this body of death?" (v. 24). Paul recognizes that his hope lies not in his efforts to do better, try harder, be more obedient. Every attempt on his part to bridge the gap between himself and God only widens it. He does not need to be more diligent; he needs to be delivered. Only God can give what human effort cannot obtain. "Thanks be to God through Jesus Christ our Lord!" (v. 25).

### GOSPEL: MATTHEW 11:25-30

New Testament scholars tell us that if we put this text under a microscope we can see where three quite different types of sayings have apparently been glued together by Matthew's editorial hand. The first saying (vv. 25-26) has all the Semitic flavor of an authentic statement of Jesus. The second saying (v. 27), however, with its talk of the revelation of the Father being known only through the Son, looks for all the world like it wandered over by mistake from the Gospel of John. That is not the case, of course, but the appearance of such gnostic-flavored "knowing" language here in Matthew is so unexpected that scholars have dubbed this verse the "Johannine thunderbolt." [14] The third saying (vv. 28-30), echoes the language of a passage from the deuterocanonical book Sirach (51:25-27).

Despite these marked differences in language and style, the various pieces of this passage somehow work together as a coherent unit. Indeed, the three sayings are woven together to form three logically linked movements of thought:

1. *The rejection of Jesus is not accidental.* The whole of chapter 11 up to this text has made it clear that the ministry of Jesus in Galilee has fallen on blind eyes and deaf ears (esp. 11:20). Why was Jesus rejected? Why did his preaching, teaching, and mighty acts produce so little in the way of results? The reason: The Father has hidden the demonstrations of the wisdom of the kingdom from "the wise and understanding and revealed them to babes" (v. 25). What appeared to be a failure, then, was actually according to God's "gracious will" (v. 26).

2. *The turn toward a new community.* In Matthew, the wisdom of the kingdom of heaven is viewed as hidden knowledge, as a kind of secret. In Jesus' ministry, this secret is "whispered" and "told in the dark" (10:27). Jesus attempted to reveal the secret of the kingdom to the cities of Israel, but they closed their ears and eyes. So now the secret will be told to a new people, those with "ears to hear" (13:9), and "nothing is covered that will not be revealed" (10:26). All of these things, Jesus says, "have been delivered to me by my Father" and will be disclosed "to any one to

whom the Son chooses to reveal him" (v. 27). This saying anticipates chap. 13, where Jesus tells the disciples, as the forerunners of the new community, "To you it has been given to know the secrets of the kingdom of heaven" (13:11).

3. *The invitation to the new community.* To whom will the secret of the kingdom be revealed? Not to the strong and self-reliant, but "to those who labor and are heavy laden" (v. 28); not to the proud and the wise, but to "babes" (v. 25); not to the self-righteous and unrepentant, but to the "poor in spirit," "those who mourn," and the "meek" (5:2-5). How shall this new community respond to the invitation? By hearing, believing, and obeying the teaching of Jesus. "Take my yoke upon you and learn from me" (v. 29). Who is the teacher? Jesus, who is himself "gentle and lowly in heart" (v. 29). What happens to those who respond? "You will find rest for your souls" (v. 29).

One is reminded by this text of the often-told incident that occurred in the early days of the civil rights movement in the southern United States, during the Montogmery, Alabama bus boycott. The leaders of the boycott discovered that an elderly black woman, known affectionately as "Mother" Pollard, was supporting the boycott, walking many miles each day instead of riding the bus. Because of her advanced age, she was encouraged by the leadership to go ahead and take the bus and to save her strength. She refused, however, saying, "My feets is tired, but my soul is rested."

Mother Pollard, and those who struggled with her, hungered for righteousness, and "blessed are those who hunger and thirst for righteousness," said Jesus, the same Jesus who also said, "Take my yoke upon you, and learn from me; for I am gentle and lowly in heart, and you will find rest for your souls" (v. 29).

# The Eighth Sunday after Pentecost

| Lutheran | Roman Catholic | Episcopal | Common Lectionary |
|---|---|---|---|
| Isa. 55:10–11 | Isa. 55:10–11 | Isa. 55:1–5, 10–13 | Exod. 2:11–22 |
| Rom. 8:18–25 | Rom. 8:18–23 | Rom. 8:9–17 | Rom. 8:9–17 |
| Matt. 13:1–9 | Matt. 13:1–23 | Matt. 13:1–9, 18–23 | Matt. 13:1–9, 18–23 |

### FIRST LESSON: ISAIAH 55:1-11

Look in the windows of most travel agencies and you will see there attractive posters that picture various "getaway" spots. The Alps, the

Rockies, the Caribbean, and various other alluring locations summon the weary to refreshment. On these posters appear skiers and swimmers, golfers and hikers, people in party clothes and people reclining in lounge chairs beside pools, all of them subtly beckoning us, "Come."

Isaiah 55 is a theological travel poster. Shifts in international power have made it possible for the Hebrews in Babylonian exile to return to their homeland, to go back to Zion, and the prophet is beckoning them to come. He envisions no ordinary trip, however. This is not to be a vacation jaunt, but a new exodus. In the first exodus, God delivered the Hebrews from captivity in Egypt by making a pathway in the sea, dry land in the waters. Now, reversing the images, the prophet announces that God intends to deliver the Hebrews from captivity in Babylon by making a pathway in the wilderness, a river of life in the dry and lifeless desert (Isa. 43:19). Moreover, the prophet calls the people back, not only to the old land, but also to a renewed relationship with God. Isaiah's travel poster does not read "Get Away," but rather "Return to the Lord" (55:7).

The power of Isaiah's call to return to a place of renewed relationship with God transcends its original historical setting and reaches out to appeal to all who are in exile. The authors of *Habits of the Heart* observed that the contemporary "consumption-oriented" life-style can be a form of exile from a life of meaning. The desperate quest for fine homes, lavish meals, and carefree leisure can become, they warned, "a form of defense against a dangerous and meaningless world. . . ."[15] Moreover, the desire to be an autonomous self, the search "for purely private fulfillment is illusory: it often ends in emptiness instead."[16]

In place of emptiness, the prophet promises a land of nourishment, a banquet spread by the free grace of God. "Why do you spend your money for that which is not bread, and your labor for that which does not satisfy? Hearken diligently to me, and at what is good . . ." (v. 2). Instead of meaninglessness, the prophet promises a place where human life is gathered into the wisdom of God. God gives humanity meaning it cannot make on its own, for "my thoughts are not your thoughts, neither are your ways my ways, says the Lord" (v. 8). The true and full meaning of human life is not to be found in technology or the acquisition of more and more data, but in relationship to the God of mercy (v. 7) whose word is authentic wisdom. God's word to humanity is a word of love (v. 3), a word that grants forgiveness (v. 7), a word that brings forth good fruit (vv. 10-11), and a word that is sure to accomplish all that it purposes to do (v. 11).

## ALTERNATIVE FIRST LESSON: EXODUS 2:11-22

On the surface, this text simply describes a series of dramatic events that occurred in the young adult life of Moses. He murders an Egyptian who was beating a Hebrew, flees to Midian when Pharaoh discovers the crime, and defends the seven daughters of Reuel, the priest of Midian, against a group of shepherds. The text closes with Moses dwelling contentedly in Midian, having been given one of Reuel's daughters as a wife.

Beneath the surface, however, the text points theologically to the mysterious workings of the will of God. Every reader of this text knows that Moses was the one God called to lead Israel from captivity, as the one who received the sacred law. How did Moses come to be this person, to occupy this special place in God's redemptive history? What forces were at work to cause the trajectory of his life to be joined with that of God's action in history?

The passage presents Moses as a person who identified strongly with the Hebrew people (v. 11), even though he had every reason to ignore their slave status and to claim privileged standing as the grandson of mighty Pharaoh (2:10). The text also portrays Moses as one who instinctively took up the cause of the victim (vv. 12, 17) and as one who refused to rest easy in any situation, but even when blessed with land and family still called himself a "sojourner" (v. 22). In short, we see in this biographical snapshot of Moses a "natural" candidate to lead the Hebrews from bondage to freedom: a man who values his Hebrew identity, who understands their sojourner status, and who takes on the cause of the oppressed.

On the other hand, though, there is much about this story that seems to occur accidentally and by chance. Moses just happens to be down at the slave camp when the Egyptian is beating the Hebrew. On any other day he might well have observed the general harshness of the slave conditions, been bothered by this, and made a mental note to take it up with Pharaoh when he got an opportunity. But on this day he encounters an act of personal violence, and he reacts in a way that changes his life. Why did he go? Why did he go that day? In Acts, Stephen said "it came into his heart to visit his brethren" (Acts 7:23). From whence did this impulse come? And what about his flight from Egypt? He could just as well have run out into the desert or up into the region of the Hittites, but he ends up in Midian instead. Midian was the place of the burning bush, the place of transforming encounter with God (Some scholars believe there was already a Yahweh cult there and that the priest of Midian, Moses' father-in-law, was its leader, see Exodus 18). And note the irony of the statement by Reuel's daughters, "An Egyptian delivered us out of the hand of the shepherds" (v. 19). This is a foreshadowing of Moses the shepherd who will deliver the flock of Israel from the hand of the Egyptians.

In other words, what places Moses at the pivot point of Israel's history is a curious mixture of predictability and chance, destiny and grace, human will and divine providence. Such a wondrous intertwining of human striving and divine intervention can only be seen in retrospect. The same is true for all faithful people. When we ask ourselves, How did we get to this place? How did we come to this moment? We can tell our stories, recount our experiences, but there is always something mysterious left over. Finally we must say, as the author of Hebrews said of Moses, "God led me here by faith" (Heb. 11:23-29).

### EPISTLE: ROMANS 8:9-17

(For those using the Lutheran or Roman Catholic lectionaries, commentary on Romans 8:18-25 may be found under The Ninth Sunday after Pentecost, pp. 60-61.)

The image to keep in mind here is that of a royal heir to the throne, say a prince who will, in time, become king. Imagine what life is like for this prince. He is not yet the king, but he is the royal child and the heir of the kingdom, and already his life is determined by these realities. What he says, what he thinks, and what he does are urgently important. If he were to rise one morning and say, "I am not yet the king, so today I will act in an unroyal fashion," it would be a foolish and shortsighted denial of his true self. His life is an anticipation of who he will eventually become. His eyes must be constantly fixed upon his inheritance, and every day he must grow toward what he will be.

A similar image governs this text from Paul. Jesus Christ is the true heir of the kingdom, the true Son of God, but Jesus Christ is not the only heir. By the grace of God, faithful people have been gathered into Christ and made "fellow heirs with Christ" (v. 17). The Holy Spirit takes out adoption papers on slaves, on orphans, on rebellious nobodies, and brings them into the family of God, making them royal children (v. 14). Every time we cry "Abba! Father!" (v. 15), every time we say "Our Father, who art in heaven," every time we pray to the God who nurses us as a mother, "it is the Spirit bearing witness with our spirit that we are children of God and heirs of God" (vv. 16-17).

To be an heir, however, is not yet to have arrived. The fullness of the kingdom still lies ahead, the full possession of freedom and the full reality of peace with God are now seen "through a mirror dimly" (1 Cor. 13:12). But if we should rise in the morning and say, "Since the kingdom is not yet here, I will live today as if there were no kingdom at all," it would be a tragic denial of who we are. As Paul states it, "You are not in the flesh, you are in the Spirit. . . . You did not receive the spirit of slavery to fall back into fear, but you have received the spirit of sonship" (vv. 9,15). Daughters and sons of God, joint heirs to the kingdom with Christ, live toward their future inheritance.

Most people live their lives as if they had no sure inheritance. They treat life as if it were a rich and capricious uncle who at any moment may cut them out of the will. So they flatter and deceive, stab rivals in the back, grab everything they can get, and behave like disowned relatives trying to manipulate themselves back into position to get their share. As columnist Mike Royko once suggested, the motto for many contemporary people is, "Where's mine?"

The glory of the gospel is that it puts an end to all of our desperate grasping. What we hunger for most has already been given to us as a gift. We are children of grace, children of God. Because we have already been promised everything, we are freed from all need to take life by force; we are free even, as Christ himself was free, to endure suffering (v. 17). As the old hymn "Children of the Heavenly King" stated: "Fear not, children, joyful stand, on the borders of your land; Christ, your Father's elder Son, bids you undismayed go on."

### GOSPEL: MATTHEW 13:1-23

A motorist lost on a country road, the old story goes, asks a farmer for directions to Centerville. "Well, you take the Village Road," says the farmer, but the motorist confesses that he does not know the Village Road. "OK, then, you turn left at Bryson's store." But the motorist has never heard of Bryson's store. So the farmer tries once again. "Go two miles north from Antioch Church." Alas, the motorist hasn't heard of the church either. "Well I can't help you then," shrugs the farmer. "You have to know something to get to Centerville."

Sometimes a person has to know something already in order to learn something new. Any novice who has ever tried to read a letter written in a foreign language, struggled with the impenetrable prose of a computer manual, or wrestled with the indecipherable symbols of a calculus textbook recognizes this truth. Some new knowledge requires a prior understanding, a framework of perception into which to place the fresh information. In the deepest possible sense, this text from Matthew 13 expresses this same truth. Who can understand the mysteries of the kingdom of heaven? Only those who are already oriented to the kingdom, only those who already believe that the kingdom has been inaugurated in Jesus, only those to whom "the secrets of the kingdom" have been given (v. 11).

The passage begins with Jesus telling the crowds a farm story about seed falling on four different types of soil, three poor and one good (vv. 2-9). A first-century crowd would have found the details of this story thoroughly unremarkable (save, of course, for the astounding good fortune of this sower. A harvest of a hundred-, sixty-, or even thirtyfold would have been the talk of the land.). In the main the story seems to be basically straight description, in fact, essentially pointless, except that Jesus hints powerfully that there is a hidden meaning in the story, but only for those who have ears to hear (v. 9).

Once the story is told, the disciples have a private conversation with Jesus in which they ask him, "Why do you speak to them in parables?" (v. 10). Note that they do not ask about the meaning of what Jesus said; they rather ask why he talks to people that way in the first place—that is, parabolically. Jesus' reponse to their question is complex, involving several enigmatic statements and a quotation from the Septuagint version of Isaiah 6:9-10 (vv. 14-15), but it boils down to this: I speak to the crowds in parables because they see and hear what I do and say, but they don't get it. Jesus then goes on to say that the disciples, by contrast, *do* get it (v. 16), and because they do they are entitled to hear a line-by-line private explanation of the parable (vv. 18-23). In other words, because the disciples know something (the basic truth of the kingdom), they are able to learn something else (the wisdom of the kingdom teachings contained in the parable). What was only a somewhat exaggerated farmer's yarn to the crowds becomes a profound manual of kingdom instruction for the disciples.

The basic force of this passage, then, is that one must believe in the kingdom, be oriented to the essential vision and truth of the kingdom, in order to see, understand, and trust the growth of the kingdom. The world measures growth in profits and losses; the kingdom measures growth in righteousness. The world measures growth in power, missile silos, and defense systems; the kingdom measures growth in meekness and gentleness. The world measures growth in domination; the kingdom measures growth in love of enemies. So, Jesus teaches in parables because the kingdom *itself* is a parable. If one believes in the parable *of* the kingdom, the parables *about* the kingdom become clear. If one does not believe, the parables appear mundane, opaque, wildly exaggerated, or even foolish. The world "sees" the presence of the kingdom and "hears" it, but does not understand it. To closed ears, the message of the kingdom sounds like bad advice and an invitation to disaster. To uncomprehending eyes, the bountiful kingdom harvest of mercy and peace looks for all the world like a crop failure, but to obedient disciples: "Blessed are your eyes, for they see, and your ears for they hear" (v. 16) and you "bear fruit and yield" (v. 23) in abundance.

# The Ninth Sunday after Pentecost

| Lutheran | Roman Catholic | Episcopal | Common Lectionary |
|---|---|---|---|
| Isa. 44:6–8 | Wisd. of Sol. 12:13, 16–19 | Wisd. of Sol. 12:13, 16–19 | Exod. 3:1–12 |
| Rom. 8:26–27 | Rom. 8:26–27 | Rom. 8:18–25 | Rom. 8:18–25 |
| Matt. 13:24–30 | Matt. 13:24–43 | Matt. 13:24–30, 36–43 | Matt. 13:24–30, 36–43 |

## FIRST LESSON: ISAIAH 44:6-8

This text appears as part of a magnificent and dramatic courtroom scene. The case is "The Peoples of the Earth vs. Yahweh"; the alleged crime is that Yahweh has falsely claimed to be the only true God. The prophet portrays Yahweh as eager for the trial to begin: "Let the nations bring their witnesses, and I'll bring mine, and all will learn that I am the Lord, and besides me there is no savior" (Isa. 43:9, 11). And who are Yahweh's witnesses? The people of Israel. Israel will take the stand and testify to the mighty deeds of God in history. Ironically, though, it is Yahweh who takes the stand first. Yahweh is the accused, but Yahweh is also the first witness, the initial one to give testimony (43:12—44:5)

When all the testimony has been taken, when all the witnesses have been heard, when all the charges and countercharges have been made, it is time for the verdict to be rendered. And who renders the verdict? Why, Yahweh, of course. Who could stand in judgment of Yahweh? Yahweh is not only the accused and the first to take the stand; Yahweh is also judge and jury. Yahweh is all in all, and Yahweh's courtroom is the only court there is. "I am the first and the last, besides me there is no god. . . . You are my witnesses! Is there a God besides me? There is no Rock; I know not any" (vv. 6-8).

Sociologist of religion Richard Fenn has observed that Christian worship is shaped like a great trial. "[O]n the Lord's Day . . . the people of God celebrate a mock trial, in which the law is read, confession and testimony obtained, and the verdict once again given as it was before all time." [17] The hymns of worship, the creeds, the reading of Scripture, the sermon, the responses of the people—all of these are the giving of testimony by the people of God that God "is the first and the last, the alpha and the omega."

This bearing of witness to the deeds of the one, true God is not restricted, of course, to the liturgy. Notice in the passage that the witness to God is in narrative form: Witnessing means "telling the story" of God's mighty acts in history. Whenever God's people speak of what God has done in their lives, whenever they teach God's story of mercy and justice to their children, or quietly tell the story to others of the power of God's claim on their lives (Deut. 6:7), they bear true witness in the great trial.

Incidentally, the verdict rendered in this great trial of God is surely the most unusual in all of legal history. Not only was God vindicated, but the accusers were transformed and blessed. The prosecuting attorney joined the defense (44:5), and even the Gentiles saw the light (49:6).

### ALTERNATIVE FIRST LESSON: EXODUS 3:1-12

This text presents the breathtaking opening scene in the call of Moses, an account that continues through 4:17. The main thrust of the text is to present the character of this God who calls Moses to decisive action, and at least five facets of this picture can be discerned:

First, God is portrayed as holy, awesome, transcendent, immeasurable, and beyond all human approaching. "Do not come near," commands the Voice in the burning bush (v. 5), and Moses is mortally afraid even to look in the direction of this Voice (v. 6; see Exod. 33:20). This text stands, then, in judgment of all casual and domesticated views of God, of all images of God as a benign force for good, something like "civic spirit." "Does anyone have the foggiest idea," wonders Annie Dillard, "what sort of power [Christians] so blithely invoke? . . . It is madness to wear ladies' straw hats and velvet hats to church; we should all be wearing crash helmets." [18] We cannot really understand the grace and mercy of God unless we take seriously the holiness of God; the God who comes to save is the God in whose very presence we should, by rights, be destroyed.

Second, the God encountered by Moses is not some new deity. This is "the God of Abraham, Isaac, and Jacob" (v. 6). This God has a history, a story, and it is the story of ongoing involvement and constant covenant with God's people. This is the God who does not forget and refuses to abandon the chosen people. This God is one who can be trusted to be steadfast, "the same yesterday and today and forever" (Heb. 13:8). The God who called Moses is the same God who called Abraham. The God who told the divine name to Moses is the same God in whose name we were baptized.

Third, the God depicted in this text is the God who hears the cries of the needy, who answers the prayers of those bruised in body and spirit. God has "seen the affliction . . . heard the cries . . . knows the sufferings," and God "will come down to deliver" (vv. 7-8). As we sing in the old hymn, "When other helpers fail and comforts flee, Help of the helpless, O abide with me."

Fourth, God is pictured as one who is disclosed in the ordinary times and places of human life. This theophany occurs "while Moses was keeping the flock" (v. 1); a contemporary equivalent might be "while Moses was waiting on a bus." And God appears in a bush, for goodness sake! Any other Near-Eastern deity would at least have stirred up a thunderstorm or caused a star to fall from heaven. Yahweh causes the nonconsuming fire of holiness to fall on a common specimen of scrub vegetation, and upon the shoulders of a shepherd minding his father-in-law's business.

Finally, despite all of the emphasis upon God's holy power and the sacred distance between God and humanity, this text also discloses a God who does not crush the human spirit under the weight of the divine command. God does not knock Moses to the earth in a flash of divine light; God *speaks* to Moses. God does not overpower Moses into silent submission; Moses finds the voice to respond, even to protest and resist God's command (v. 11). Moses is not a robot, a puppet; he is called to be a servant. God wants Moses to be the instrument for the liberation of Israel, and God does not take away Moses' human freedom for the sake of theirs.

## EPISTLE: ROMANS 8:18-27

It is, of course, a terribly anthropomorphic way to pose the question, but what do you suppose faithful prayers sound like on the ear of God? Around the clock people utter prayers for all sorts of things—prayers beside sickbeds and gravesides, prayers for health and prayers for gentle death, prayers for the hungry and prayers for the troubled in spirit, prayers for the lonely and prayers for those who have lost their way, prayers for presidents and prime ministers and prayers for the homeless. What do these prayers sound like when they strike the divine ear? According to Paul, they sound like *groans* (v. 23).

At the point in Romans where this text appears, Paul has been discussing the Christian life in the most hopeful and positive of ways. Christians, he says, have been "set free" (8:2) and possess "life and peace" (8:6). They are "heirs of God" and will be "glorified with Christ" (8:17). There is a subtle danger, Paul knows, in such talk. Christians are always prone to imagine that the true mark of faith is a numb cheeriness, oblivious to the pain and suffering in life. Someone is always trying to take the cross out of the sanctuary and put up a "smiley face" in its place.

So Paul turns quickly from talking about the joyful life in the Spirit to a discussion of the place of suffering in the world. At the base of the Statue of Liberty in New York harbor is a tablet inscribed with a poem by Emma Lazarus that reads in part: "Give me your tired, your poor, your huddled masses yearning to breathe free. . . .'' According to Paul, it is not just the tired, poor, and huddled masses that yearn to be free; it is the whole creation "waiting with eager longing" for liberation (v. 19). Suffering and decay are woven into the fabric of creation, not as punishment or through any "fault" of nature (v. 20), but so that the whole created order might strain forward in the gloom, searching for a glimmer of hope. To put it theologically, the brokenness of creation is a *prayer* to God for deliverance, and the sound of that prayer is "groaning" (v. 22).

The mournful prayer of creation is joined by the groaning prayers of Christians (v. 23). The byword of the children of God is not "Smile, God loves you!" but prayerful yearning for the age to come, inward groaning (v. 23) born of suffering, pleading cries for the redemptive presence of God: "Come, Lord Jesus" (Rev. 22:20). When Christian people look at the world with discernment they do not see many signs of God's victory in Christ. Instead they see homeless people, grieving people, children starving, power brokers in charge of the world, and wheelchair ramps leading even into the sanctuaries where God's victory is proclaimed. Such visions leave us only two choices: resignation or hope. Were it not for what we have seen and experienced in Christ, our options would be reduced to one woeful alternative. But because of the "foretaste" of the resurrection, we hope, and "in this hope we were saved" (v. 24). And so, we "wait with patience" (v. 25) and prayerfully groan.

Our groaning is so deep and so inarticulate that it would not be prayer at all if it were not for the Spirit's help. "We don't know how to pray as we ought" (v. 26) and so the Spirit gathers our yearning needs into speech before God. By the grace of God our groans become prayers, our prayers become the will of God (v. 27), and our hopes for redemption become realized.

## GOSPEL: MATTHEW 13:24-43

This passage repeats the pattern, already established earlier in the chapter, of a parable being told by Jesus to the crowds, and then the disciples pulling Jesus aside to get the inside information about its meaning. This, again, reflects Matthew's theological emphasis that a parable, like the kingdom itself, is presented for all the world to hear, but only the faithful have access to its full meaning. The passage includes the parable of the weeds and the wheat (vv. 24-30) followed by two brief parables of expansion (the mustard seed and the leaven—vv. 31-33), all spoken in public to the crowds. Then Matthew tells the reader, backing it up with a quotation from Psalm 78:2, that the purpose of Jesus' parables was to "utter what has been hidden since the foundation of the world" (vv. 34-35). Finally Jesus huddles privately with the disciples and gives them an elaborate allegorical

interpretation of the "hidden" meaning of the weeds and wheat parable
(vv. 36-43). So, once more Matthew's Jesus strides across the stage speaking
his parabolic lines to the big theater audience, who hear what he says but
haven't the foggiest idea what he means. Then Jesus leans over to his
friends on the front row and whispers the secret meaning (see 13:11).

Most scholars agree that this entire string of sayings can best be understood against the backdrop of a problem in Matthew's own church.
Jesus was speaking kingdom *parables*, but Matthew was writing church
*polity*. What was the situation in Matthew's church? Risking an anach-
ronism, we can say that Matthew's church was probably as close as one
gets in the New Testament to what a contemporary person would call a
"suburban church." The evidence is strong that Matthew's congregation
lived in or near a city, were people of mixed cultural backgrounds, and
were fairly well-to-do economically.[19] Their main problem, then, was not
poverty, but purity. All around them were rival religions, pagan religions,
and people with no religion at all. What's more, there were, in their own
"pews," people of great faith and people of little faith, persons of merciful
spirit and persons of contentious spirit, saints with steady obedience and
sinners with blushingly lax morals. In short, Matthew's church was much
like many churches today, set down in the midst of a bewilderingly plu-
ralistic society and composed of members both weak and strong, devout
and nonchalant, eager to hear the Word and ready to drift off to sleep
during the sermon, folks prepared to send their money and themselves into
all the world for mission and also folks prepared to bury their talents in
the backyard and wash their hands of the whole thing. In other words: the
*real* church.

Presumably the leaders of Matthews' church were able to do very little
about the impurities in the world, but they could exercise discipline in the
church. They couldn't do much about cleaning up the mess in society, but
they could attempt to clean up the mess in the ecclesiatical house. The
only question was, should they? That's the key question of this passage.
The parable of the weeds and the wheat pictures the world (and the church)
as a vast field in which the Lord has sown good seed (vv. 24, 37). So far,
so good. But secretly, while everyone was asleep, an enemy sowed bad
seed in the field, and when the plants began to sprout, there were grain
and weeds, good and bad, all mixed up together—just like Matthew's
church. The servants wonder if they should root out the weeds, but the
answer, given an eschatological twist in vv. 36-43, is "No, the time is not
right. If you try to uproot the weeds now, you may destroy the grain as
well. Wait until the harvest, and then Lord will separate the weeds and
the grain in a dramatic and purifying way."

The text, then, conveys confident good news to the church. The victory of God's kingdom, even the effectiveness of the church, is not dependent upon human efforts to keep the church pure. The parable of the weeds and the wheat is primarily a call to remember that ultimately the harvest and the victory belong to God and depend alone upon God's patient working in the world. This understanding is embodied in what Pope John XXIII said to himself each night as he ended his prayers, "But who governs the church? You or the Holy Spirit? Very well, then, go to sleep, Angelo." [20]

If this were the only message of this text, however, it could well encourage inattentiveness and ethical laxity. The moral lesson of the parable could well be, "Don't do anything. Go with the flow; let the weeds grow with the grain; and sit on your hands waiting for God to take care of it in the end." That is why, between the parable of the weeds and the wheat and its interpretation, come the twin parables of the mustard seed and the leaven. In both of these parables the kingdom of heaven is compared to something small and hidden (a mustard seed, a bit of leaven) which grows and spreads to become large and pervasive. Putting the three parables together, then, the vocation of kingdom people is not to spend their time rooting out evil and burning up iniquity. That task finally requires a discernment belonging only to God. The vocation of kingdom people, rather, is patiently to go about the merciful work of the kingdom. Compared to the churning confusion of the world's energies, this seems like small and weak activity to be sure. But, like the mustard seed and the leaven, the work of the kingdom, when all is said and done, is the only thing that really counts.

# Notes

1. Anne Tyler, *Dinner at the Homesick Restaurant* (New York: Berkeley Books, 1982), 18.

2. F. Robert Rodman, *Keeping Hope Alive: On Becoming a Psychotherapist* (New York: Harper & Row, 1986), 5.

3. T. S. Eliot, *Murder in the Cathedral*, in *The Complete Plays of T. S. Eliot* (New York: Harcourt, Brace & World, 1967), 30.

4. W. Dow Edgerton, "The Binding of Isaac," *Theology Today* 44/2 (1987): 207.

5. "Letter to Diognetus," *Early Christian Fathers, The Library of Christian Classics*, vol. 1, translated and edited by Cyril C. Richardson (Philadelphia: Westminster Press, 1953), 216–18, as quoted in William H. Willimon, *What's Right with the Church* (San Francisco: Harper & Row, 1985), 73–74.

6. John H. Leith, *The Reformed Imperative: What the Church Has to Say That No One Else Can Say* (Philadelphia: Westminster Press, 1988), 65.

7. Quoted by William H. Willimon in *Sighing for Eden: Sin, Evil, and the Christian Faith* (Nashville: Abingdon Press, 1985), 24.

8. Quoted by Barbara K. Lundblad in "Staying Where You Are," a sermon preached on the Lutheran Series of "The Protestant Hour" radio program.

9. Quoted by William Muehl in *Why Preach? Why Listen?* (Philadelphia: Fortress Press, 1986), 60.

10. Stanley Hauerwas, "Hating Mothers as the Way to Peace," *Journal for Preachers* 11/4 (Pentecost 1988): 18.

11. Peter DeVries, *Comfort Me with Apples* (Boston: Little, Brown, 1956), 101.

12. Quoted by William Muehl in *Why Preach? Why Listen?* (Philadelphia: Fortress Press, 1986), 63.

13. Ernst Käsemann, *Commentary on Romans* (Grand Rapids, Mich.: Wm. B. Eerdmans, 1980), 203.

14. David Hill, *The Gospel of Matthew*, The New Century Bible Commentary (Grand Rapids, Mich.: Wm. B. Eerdmans, 1972), 204.

15. Robert N. Bellah, et al., *Habits of the Heart: Individualism and Commitment in American Life* (Berkeley, Los Angeles, London: University of California Press, 1985), 291.

16. Ibid., 163.

17. Richard K. Fenn, *Liturgies and Trials* (New York: Pilgrim Press, 1982), 27.

18. Annie Dillard, *Teaching a Stone to Talk: Expeditions and Encounters* (New York: Harper & Row, 1982), 40.

19. See, for example, the discussion of Matthew's community in Jack Dean Kingsbury, *Matthew as Story* (Philadelphia: Fortress Press, 1986), 120–133.

20. Peter Nichols, *Politics of the Vatican* (New York: Praeger, 1968), 109, as quoted in William Willimon, *What's Right with the Church* (San Francisco: Harper & Row, 1985), 48.